"I found this book to be a practical guide on how to succeed in an office environment by overcoming the obstacles of office politics."
—Governor Terry E. Branstad, President and CEO, Des Moines University; Governor of the State of Iowa (1983-1999)

"Timothy Johnson's *GUST* is like a breath of fresh air, offering new insights into dealing with the age old problem of office politics. With deep characters we all can relate to, and situations that happen in every environment, this book provides solutions for dealing with the complex corporate environment with straightforward advice and solutions based in the real world."
—Phil Gerbyshak, author, *10 Ways to Make it Great!*

"Timothy Johnson has a gift for using interesting characters and their stories in order to teach us how to be successful in our organizations. In his latest business fable, *GUST,* he goes beyond just telling us why office politics happen to sharing useful tips to cope when colleagues turn out to be "snakes, ostriches, or bears." This book is a great training tool for both employees and managers to learn what to do when you are unable to get the resources you need. It also is appropriate for college professors teaching strategy, decision-making, marketing, or management to help students learn how to function effectively in the work world."
—Delaney J. Kirk, Ph.D., Professor of Management, Drake University; author, *Taking Back the Classroom: Tips for the College Professor on Becoming a More Effective Teacher*

D1457279

1

"While you can't avoid office politics, deciding not to play in this game is not an option. In this simple, yet powerful story on office politics, Timothy provides you a framework to succeed in the workplace. When I completed reading the book, I felt like I could have used Liz's help many times in the past!"
—Rajesh Setty, Entrepreneur; author, *Beyond Code*

"Timothy has presented a compelling fable that gives the up and coming leader a crash course in recognizing and overcoming destructive and dysfunctional work environments. His advice is spot on, as well as his clever characterizations of the political players we've all encountered at one time or another. A great read!"
—Terry St. Marie, Senior Vice President of Operations, Bresnan Communications

"If I read this book the day I went into business, my entire career would have been more remarkable, the companies and the people I worked with and for would have been so much easier to comprehend and communicate with. *GUST* is a course in how to understand your environment. Every business person, from analyst to creative director, should read it and keep a copy for quick reference when a political roadblock occurs. Whole companies should read this book together."
—Liz Strauss, On-line Publisher, Successful-Blog

"People are political. Office politics are a given. How will you respond? *GUST* makes sense of office politics for everyone by making a story all of us can relate to and learn from. Timothy Johnson has seen nearly every kind of office battle you can imagine. The good news: he's sharing a very wise tale full of essential lessons you and your office need! Don't just read *GUST* by yourself. Have all the "political animals" you know read it too!"
—Mike Wagner, President, White Rabbit Group

2

GUST

The "Tale" Wind of Office Politics

ISBN 978-1-934417-00-3

Acknowledgements

Shannon, Lauren, and Abby – How can I thank you enough for being my sanctuary of sanity when I don't have to deal with office politics?

My extended family and close friends – You have listened to all my stories over the years; I hope this puts them into greater context.

Catherine Staub and the team at Lexicon – Thank you for a delightful publishing experience.

Delaney Kirk, Mike Wagner, Mike Sansone, Steve Farber, Phil Gerbyshak, Terry St. Marie, Liz Strauss, and Roger von Oech – You've all inspired my work and helped to reshape my thinking. My professional life would not be complete without you.

Brian Amick – Your friendship continues to propel me forward; the pep talks and Starbucks runs didn't hurt either.

Jon Grannis, Judy Beswick, Rod Leaverton, Eric Orcutt, Ted Sheridan and others who had an active hand in shaping this text – Your input and insights helped to make this a much better product than I could have ever produced alone.

Twelve years of students and twenty years of coworkers and clients – Thanks for just being you—the good, the bad, the inspiration.

God – Thanks for making us all different; it keeps things interesting and provides me with plenty of fodder for writing.

Introduction

Office politics. Ugh.

Is that how you feel about politics? Many people experience office politics on a daily basis, some without even knowing it. Before you start reading this book, see if any of the following sound familiar:

- "The rug is pulled out from underneath me all the time. Just when I think I'm making progress, somebody pulls some underhanded stunt, leaving me in a bind."

- "I hate politics. I don't want to deal with it. People who play politics are not nice individuals; they're all just trouble-makers. Why can't people just get along?"

- "There are no politics in my company. Sure… things slow us down, but people are generally cooperative… although, there was that one time…."

- "Just let me at 'em. They'll wish they never crossed my path in the first place."

- "I generally avoid politics by just doing everything myself. Yes, I'm overworked and stressed, and sometimes my ideas get pulled after they are implemented because I didn't involve others, but it's just easier to carry the load by myself. Better to ask forgiveness than wait for approval, right?"

In my experience as a consultant, coach, and instructor, I've run across many upwardly mobile professionals who are still unequipped to handle the issues surrounding office politics. These professionals, who are very adept at analyzing finances, balancing giant spreadsheets, and creating complex Gantt charts for multi-million dollar programs, find themselves woefully inept at managing the perceptions and expectations of people. They carry with them a myriad of myths and misconceptions about office politics.

Do you fit that description? Are you still on the first half of your career life cycle? Have you worked your way into junior or middle management? Do you find yourself befuddled with "how the game is played"? Do you find that the executives above you are largely unhelpful (or even clueless) with regards to the office politics that are played within your team, department, or organization? It is for you that I have written this book.

Technically speaking, I did not write this book; I merely blended a collection of realities into story form. It is a culmination of real events from the stories of hundreds of people. No one aspect of this business fable is fiction. The characters' names have been created, but they are merely fictional vehicles that I'm using to act out real human drama. As you read this book, you will make discoveries about the process of office politics. You likely will see yourself and some of your coworkers within these pages. You will learn something about how you and they approach the art of office politics. You will learn to step back and take a "big picture view" of the situation, the players, and the reasons behind the behaviors. You may have to admit your fears about office politics: that you will make matters worse, that you will compromise your morals, that you will soil your reputation, or that you will hurt somebody's feelings. These fears can paralyze you from becoming the professional you were meant to be.

Office politics are real. If you work in a professional environment and think you can avoid politics, you're not being honest with yourself or others. Even the attempt to withdraw from politics is, in itself, a declaration of how you "play the game." You become an office politician by default. Let's face facts: you may not be able to change others' behaviors, nor can you probably change the entire culture of your organization. But you can impact how YOU deal with the office politics which YOU have to handle. And if you want to face up to the battles of office politics and learn how to engage more proactively and intelligently, then this book is written for you. One disclaimer, though: while this book is a short-read business fable, learning politics is a lifelong process that takes practice.

Engaging in office politics does not mean that you must become mean-spirited. It does not mean that you have to begin stabbing people in the back for your own gains. It does mean, however, that you need to learn and practice some basic survival skills, things you should have been learning all along. Office politics in and of themselves are not evil. This book uses a GUST of wind as its metaphor for office politics. A gentle breeze can clear the air. The wind can usher in weather fronts that bring moisture or sunshine. The wind can be harnessed to produce electricity. The wind, at its worst, comes in the form of tornadoes and hurricanes. The wind can also spur dangerous wildfires. In the most damaging cases, the wind's effects are forewarned to those who may be impacted. In the same way, office politics can be used to further the team and the organization to achieve a greater good and to accomplish new heights. Alternatively, office politics can be used to decimate careers and ruin productivity. The power to harness politics, then, comes from the level of control we decide to exert over our own areas of influence, and how we are able to maintain those relationships within our personal and professional environments.

Keep an open mind when reading this book. While it is a business book, some elements of faith, values, and beliefs were integrated. Not in a way that is intended to be condescending or preachy, but in order to demonstrate that politics do not need to undermine values systems, regardless of which religion (if any) you practice. The game of office politics acknowledges no one specific industry, religion, race, gender, or culture. We all play the game, whether we know it or not. This book is designed to provide you with the tools to play the game with a little clearer perspective of what is going on around you. Those skills alone should contribute to your effectiveness and satisfaction in the workplace. You will also learn to dispel some of the myths surrounding office politics … the roadblocks that have kept you from engaging in the game. When you read about the characters from the fictional company of **REV**:Elation, my hope is that you will give that nodding grin, saying, "Ah yes, I've been there, too."

At the end of the book, there are five appendices, or Tale Winds as they've been tagged. In Tale Wind 1, there is a character map to explain a little more about each character's depth and values. In Tale Wind 2, there is a "quick reference" for all of the acronyms and charts throughout the book. Tale Wind 3 contains a template for you to follow as you learn the process of managing your own political challenges each day. Tale Wind 4 gives some additional acknowledgements to those who have unwittingly inspired me. Tale Wind 5 relates to the discussion between Liz and Anne in the Epilogue, and helps you determine your BOAT factor as you take office politics management to an organizational level.

Enjoy the journey. My hope is that you come away with some tips to make your work experience more enjoyable and productive.

Timothy Johnson
Spring 2007

"I'll take a tall mocha, non-fat, double shot, medium foam."

Frank Truman had not varied his order at this coffee shop for the better part of 12 years. This morning, he found himself annoyed that no barista existed who consistently remembered what he liked and would fix it correctly for him. He had read about coffee shops where the staff recognized long-time customers and had their favorites waiting before they even vocalized their desires. On this particular morning, ordering his caffeinated drink of choice felt like repetitively stating the obvious.

Especially today—anticipating his meeting with Vic Elliott—Frank did not have the patience to wait a moment longer. Victor was **REV**:Elation's senior product designer, but Vic and Frank had known each other for about 25 years. The same age, both had started their careers in the same department at the same company. Vic was a California boy, educated in the shadow of Silicon Valley's burgeoning technology industries. Frank was a Midwesterner, conservative and perceptive. Enduring the "boss from hell" together made them fast allies. Working together for the next several months solidified their friendship. Various career moves and promotions separated them professionally, but they stayed in close contact.

A few years later, Frank was offered the Chief Executive Officer position at a privately owned home products corporation that had been tightly run by the same family for decades. The founder's daughter no longer had an interest in the day-to-day operations, and her move to the Chairwoman's role paved the way for Frank to take the helm. One of his first changes was a reimaging and rebranding of the organization, and **REV**:Elation, Inc. was born. Another change Frank knew he needed to make was a shake up in the product design area, and he knew exactly whom he wanted to design the company's top products. The hiring process was a mere formality, and Vic was now approaching his tenth anniversary with the firm. In the years since, Frank and Vic had moved **REV**:Elation to the top of the industry with lines in health and beauty, home improvement products, and lifestyle publishing. The explosion of business had brought with it many growing pains, but Frank considered them normal casualties of success.

"Sir? Sir???" The squeaky-voiced young man behind the counter brought Frank back to his current surroundings. "Your mocha is ready. Double foam, half shot … right?"

"Well, not exactly…" Frank caught the blank stare on the youth's face. "Oh, never mind." He grabbed his travel mug and headed out the door to the elevator bank, muttering about the state of America's budding (or wilting) workforce.

Vic was waiting in Frank's office. Before he could apologize or explain the delay, he could sense something was amiss with Vic. His whole disposition was different. Body language, facial expression, energy level—all were out of the norm from what he had recently observed in his colleague.

"You're late, Frank," Victor lobbed, somewhat lightheartedly. "Another bumbling barista?"

"What's with you?" Frank changed the subject. "I haven't seen you like this in years. What gives?"

The secret of a long friendship, generally, is that there are no secrets. Victor was not looking forward to what was coming next, but he knew that the reward at the end of this bumpy ride would be worth it. He decided to cut to the chase.

"Frank, I'm leaving *REV*:Elation. I've found a position at a young start-up firm, and I start at the beginning of the month."

"Leaving? Don't be ridiculous. *REV*:Elation is hammering the competition right now. What could be worth leaving for? I thought you and I were together forever here."

"This is too good of an opportunity to pass up, Frank. The pay is a little less than what I'm making here, but the long-term rewards have great potential. It's also a smaller firm, a little more entrepreneurial. Some new products. New faces. New industry. New projects." It was a good line, but something in Victor's face and voice weren't adding up. Frank scrutinized his colleague for about ten seconds before responding.

"Cut the crap, Vic. We've both put too much into this company, and we've known each other too long. What's really behind this?" Frank had a very keen eye for inconsistency.

Vic paused for a moment. He really had hoped to avoid the real reasons for his decision. Nevertheless, a friendship spanning more than two decades does not leave much room for hiding anything. He took a deep breath.

"Frank, *REV*:Elation has changed over the past few years. You've changed. I've changed. The things that brought me to this organization have faded as the company has grown. There are now certain people here who don't share the vision that we had when you recruited me to come here."

Frank stared a few moments longer at Vic. "Look, if this is about that conflict at the executive product launch meeting last week …"

"It's not just about that," Vic injected quickly. "It's about everything. The lying. The backstabbing. The games. The hidden agendas. The ulterior motives. You're not running a company here. You're running a daycare center, and I want off the playground."

"I'm not sure what you're getting at," Frank said, steadying his voice. He could feel his blood pressure rising in defense.

"Frank, you're one of the smartest men I know. You're also an innovative entrepreneur who has built an enterprise. And you're a go-getter, driven harder and faster than most. So it amazes me that you do not see what is happening right under your nose!" Vic raised his volume slightly, incredulous that an executive could be so dense.

"No, Vic, tell me what is happening. Obviously, taking this company to the top of our industry isn't enough of a credibility-builder for you. Please tell me what I'm doing wrong."

"OK, *that* kind of tone won't get you very far with me," Vic was now clearly impatient. "And believe it or not, it's not all about you. I never said you specifically were doing anything wrong. The politics around here are stifling. You have a Chief Operating Officer who runs the product engineering division like some kind of organized crime family. The Director of Marketing is the black hole of information. That consultant who slithers around here acts like she runs the joint. Don't even get me started about the so-called Help Desk Manager." Vic paused to regain his composure. "And you have done nothing to remedy any of this. It reminds me of our first job … remember that?"

"The politics here aren't *that* bad," interjected Frank. "They exist everywhere. You just need to be a little better at handling people, Vic that's all … more flexible … roll with the punches. Besides, I've never had a problem with any of these people."

"That's because you're the flippin' CEO, dude!" Vic's dated West Coast vernacular surfaced occasionally when he became excited. "Did it ever occur to you that they present a different face, a different story, a different perception to you because you're the guy in charge? How can you not see what is happening here? Our company is successful—for now. If things don't change, it won't be for long. I've already heard rumblings about unhappy wholesalers and distributors. I don't want to be here when things implode."

Frank started to speak but paused, thinking that anything he said at this point would just fuel the fire. He decided to ask a simple question, "Why do you think this company will implode?"

Victor took a deep breath. "Frank, your early vision for *REV*:Elation was one of an entrepreneur. You were on a mission to accomplish something great. I loved that vision, and together we have taken this company to the top. Now that we're here, it seems that people want to stake out their turf and get what they think they're entitled to. I have a lot of my career left before retirement, Frank. I still want to accomplish something great."

"But Vic, you have accomplished great things." Unfortunately, Frank's word choice backfired.

"Frank, nobody wants their greatest accomplishments to be past tense." Vic's response seemed to fly right past Frank, who shifted into hurry-up-and-smooth-this-over executive mode.

"OK, OK, Victor, I'll talk to a few people. We'll get this taken care of. You can't go. We need you here. You can still accomplish great things. This company will not implode."

Vic shook his head sadly. Clearly this wasn't the first time he had heard this promise.

"I hope you wake up soon, Frank," he said. "Before it's too late. I'll have my desk cleared out by the end of next week. I've already been preparing my product launch project team to take on some of my responsibilities, although I've not told them why." Vic stood up to leave.

"This isn't over yet," Frank began.

"I hope it's not, for you or for *REV*:Elation. Tell you what, Frank; give me a call in a couple of months. We'll get together for coffee. A new shop just opened that knows how to make a *real* mocha."

Vic left Frank standing alone in his office, processing what he had just heard. Frank's first thoughts were denial, but he could no longer turn a blind eye to what Vic had told him. While he didn't want to admit it, he knew it was true. Things had changed at *REV*:Elation, and not for the better. It was clear that Victor had given this a lot of thought, and he definitely had made up his mind.

For once, Frank Truman was at a loss. Simply firing troublemakers at random would hardly solve anything. The culture at **REV**:Elation certainly would not support that kind of radical action. He needed help. But who? Who could get at the heart of the political issues and problems he knew was crippling his company?

That's when the idea hit Frank. He hit the intercom button to his administrative assistant.

"Bonnie, look up Liz Meredith and set up a call as soon as possible. You may have to do a little hunting. I don't know if my contact information on her is current. Clear my schedule when you find her."

Chapter 2

Liz Meredith was looking forward to a break. Not just a break, but the mother-of-all-vacations break. She sighed as she looked at the newspaper headline.

"Maleva-Calc execs indicted on 138 counts of fraud," she read aloud to no one in particular, although her cat, Mac (short for Machiavelli) perked up ever-so slightly at the sound of her voice. She read through the article, reassured that her name was not mentioned. At some point, somebody might put two and two together and figure out that she was the "hired mole" who had investigated and turned over the evidence of the deep-rooted corruption within the corporation. With the mass exodus of employees and management staff from Maleva-Calc at this point, though, her sudden disappearance would go unnoticed for weeks, probably even months, as the feds, lawyers, and remaining cooperative employees worked together to sort things out.

Liz had developed a love-hate relationship with her chosen career path. On the positive side, being a private corporate investigator provided her with opportunities to experience numerous organizations, be exposed to various industries, and observe individuals over the spectrum of human behavior. Still, after she uncovered what she was hired to investigate (and she *always* was successful at doing so), she felt more than a twinge of guilt over the effects her work had on the innocent victims who either had no idea what was going on within their own walls or knew but didn't have the power to change things. Hundreds of Maleva-Calc employees would lose their jobs, their benefits, their retirement security, and (in the case of some unscrupulous executives) their freedom.

Just once, she thought, *I would love to investigate something that would result in a positive change.*

"I need a shower," she informed Mac, who purred indifferently at her plans and plopped on a windowsill to absorb the warmth of the morning sun. The statement of her intentions was more of an editorial observation following her 18-month "project" than it was a motivation to start her morning ritual. She was compensated very well for producing the results she did, but at this point in her career, money did not seem as relevant as it had 20 years ago. Given her success and her "covert reputation" in her field, she had her choice of projects as well as ample funds to retire any time she wanted.

The phone rang as Liz was in the cycle of dry-curl-style while simultaneously applying her makeup. Muttering something about her multitasking ability only going so far, she managed to pick up and hold the phone with her forearm while corralling the jungle of appearance-enhancing products that had overtaken her bathroom.

"Hello?" Liz's tone was cordial and pleasant, even if her feelings about the interruption were anything but that.

"Ms. Meredith?" asked a professional-sounding woman on the other end.

"Speaking."

"I have Frank Truman on the line. Please hold for a moment. Thank you."

Now there's a blast from the past, thought Liz, as a man's voice came through the receiver.

"Liz?"

"Frank! What's it been? Eight years? Nine?"

"Too long, Liz. And it's taken me over two weeks just to track you down."

"How are you doing? What's going on?" Liz never missed the chance to cut to the chase, even with old friends. "You still playing corporate cog?"

"I was wondering if you were in the middle of championing corporate justice or if you were between projects. I could really use your help." Frank surprised himself and Liz by zipping to the bottom line.

"Frank, I'd love to see you again and catch up, but I've just completed a very intense investigation, and I really need some recharge time. You're not in trouble, are you?"

"If 'in trouble' means impending investigation for corporate fraud, then the answer is no. We're doing fine here at *REV*: Elation. If 'in trouble' means that we appear to have a huge problem with office politics that's been going on right under my nose for years, and it's now exploding in my face, then the answer is an emphatic yes!" Liz was amused by Frank's rambling animation when he was passionate about an issue.

"Office politics? You want me to come and referee a bunch of dysfunctional managers who can't play nice in the same corporate sandbox?" Liz tried not to sound too incredulous.

"Liz, it's more than playing referee. I just lost my top product designer due to office politics. I trust his judgment, especially now that he's gone. It didn't take me very long to figure out that he was right. And worse yet, it didn't take me long to realize that his accusation that I was part of the problem was also correct. Because of his departure, our latest product launch is in serious jeopardy."

"So, solve it, Frank! You're a bright guy. Charismatic leader. You were born to do this stuff. It's in your blood."

"I wish I could. This one is bigger than I am. Plus, I need an outsider's viewpoint. I'm too enmeshed in all of this stuff day in and day out. I think my credibility as the CEO is being undermined by the very culture I helped create."

Liz sighed. "If I had a dollar for every CEO who tried to pick me up with that tired old line," she teased.

"What will it take to get you here, Liz? Money is no object," interjected Frank, ignoring her gentle ribbing. "Name your price."

"OK, I want an all expenses paid six-month-long cruise when this is done, and I want you to hold my cell phone and my PDA hostage until I return."

"Are you serious?" Frank sounded surprised at the terms of this agreement.

"I'll let you know when I get there. Give me the information, and I'll be there a week from Monday. That should give me time to take care of a couple of things around here." Liz had learned to turn on a dime due to the nature of her career.

"Liz, you're a saint! I owe you for this one," Frank said, his tone notably appreciative.

"Save the accolades until I figure out how to make your people get along with each other."

Frank and Liz agreed that the best cover for her would be as Vic Elliott's replacement, leading the product launch project team. While Liz did not have the product design expertise that Vic had, Frank was confident that he could spin the hiring decision however he needed to make it sound plausible. Additionally, with her investigative background, Liz could sound the part as much or as little as she desired and Frank needed. There might be some backlash from the team that Vic had managed, questioning why none of them had been moved into his role, but that was a bridge he would cross only if necessary.

For most of the day the following Monday and Tuesday, Frank met Liz off-site to fill her in on the key players in his organization and their roles, the project she would be leading, and some of the "issues" he was observing. His descriptions were fairly direct yet not extremely detailed, leaving Liz to assume that Frank's self-assessment of being out of touch was somewhat accurate.

When she arrived at the **REV**:Elation headquarters on Wednesday, Liz was escorted through some of the new employee formalities within Human Resources. As she stepped onto the elevator that would transport her to her new project team, her new role, and her new cover, she noticed a man already on the elevator animatedly talking on his cell phone. He was medium-height and had a stocky build, and he appeared to be a couple of years older than Liz. His rounded face and piercing eyes were framed by a head of silver hair with shocks of reddish-orange, hinting at his younger days.

I wish people would be more considerate of their mobile phone manners, she thought as the door closed. While she disliked being forced to eavesdrop on a conversation, something about this stranger's side of the dialogue caught her attention. It wasn't only his inconsiderate ranting and raving in her presence that led her to listen in, but the content of what he was saying to the poor recipient on the other end.

"You are worthless!" the man spewed into the phone receiver. "Why **REV**:Elation keeps your sorry tail on the payroll is beyond me, but you can be thankful that your product team isn't under my control … at least for now!" His face became redder with each word, and his hair seemed to stand on end at the strangest angle, almost making it appear as if he had the horns of a demonic troll.

For the next thirty seconds, Liz unwillingly listened to an expletive-laden berating worse than anything she'd ever heard in a corporate setting. She attempted to make her presence noticed in subtle ways, but the man was intently focused on lambasting the unlucky person on the other end of the call.

Eventually, the elevator arrived at Liz's floor, and she was grateful when the door opened, allowing her to escape the verbal barrage. As she made her way to her new office, she began to understand the urgency behind Frank's request.

"Houston, we have a problem," she mused to herself. Then she grinned ever so slightly at the prospect of taking on this new challenge. She looked forward to matching a name to the elevator demon.

Chapter 3

"I'm sorry, Dee, but I can't share any of the information from the division's offsite strategy meeting," Mark Washington said, glad this was a phone conversation so the person on the other end of the line couldn't see the smirk on his face.

"Look, Mark, you said at the last managers' meeting that you would provide me with that data."

"You must have misunderstood me, Dee. I'm quite confident I would never make such a comment. And unfortunately for you, those meetings are so dry and boring that nobody ever writes anything down that would allow you to prove it."

"You and I both know that we cannot get this project implemented without that information," Dee Connors raised her voice ever so slightly. "You don't want to be the one blamed for derailing *REV*:Elation's biggest product launch, do you?"

"Yeah, right, Dee. I highly doubt that *REV*:Elation will go belly-up if I refuse to share need-to-know information with somebody who is *obviously* at a level where she doesn't need to know."

Mark's choice of tone and words always set Dee on edge. If it had been technically possible for her to reach through the phone at that exact moment, Mark probably would have ceased to exist in the employee database. Vic had directed Dee to obtain this information from Mark, and she'd been trying for weeks. Before he left the company, Vic had even attempted to expedite the request when it appeared Mark wasn't cooperating. Mark knew he had the upper hand with Vic out of the way. Both Dee and Mark knew that Vic's replacement had come from outside the company. There would be no way anyone new could navigate the organizational relationships in time to obtain the notes Dee needed. That was exactly how Mark wanted to keep it.

"Mark, you promised Vic last month that you would share that information with me!" Dee again tried valiantly to find a hot button that would motivate him to share what she needed.

"Well, Vic is no longer with us, is he?"

"For the last time, what's in that information that you don't want me to see?" Dee tried one more approach. "I've seen notes on these meetings before. I've been invited as a guest to one or two of them. There has never been anything so damaging that any person in the company should not be allowed to see it."

"Nice try, Dee. If I tell you what is so damaging, as you put it, I may as well give you the whole document. How stupid do you think I am?"

"What's the scale of measurement?"

"That's going to cost you, Connors. I think this conversation is going nowhere. Good luck trying to get your hands on this information."

Click.

Mark was known for being difficult, but Dee was kicking herself for verbalizing too many thoughts she should have kept to herself. She looked down at her phone, noticed the voice mail light was blinking, and she pressed the button to listen to her messages. There was a broadcast message from a Liz Meredith, introducing herself as Vic Elliott's replacement. There would be a project team meeting at 3:00 that afternoon in the East Conference Room so the team could meet Liz, and she could get acquainted with them.

Delightful, Dee thought sarcastically. *Just the way to ruin an otherwise awful day.*

. . .

"May I talk to you for a minute, Eve?" Anne Ericsen poked her head into her supervisor's cube.

Eve Uhlwich glanced up, pasted on a forced smile, and gestured for Anne to have a seat on the opposite side of her desk.

"What may I do for you today, Anne?" Eve's low monotone voice drawled in an attempt to fake interest in her subordinate's request, but Eve generally came across as being ambivalent to those around her, so the effort was insincere at best.

"Well, Eve, as you may remember, we discussed my career advancement at my last performance appraisal. I just saw the department's promotion list and noticed my name wasn't on it," Anne said, attempting to keep her voice steady as she usually did. Underneath, however, she was seething over another lost opportunity to move up in the organization. She knew she must not let her emotions show, though, especially to her often-antagonizing boss.

"And what was your question, specifically?" Eve countered.

What is my question? thought Anne. *She's got to be kidding!* Still, Anne knew she couldn't reveal how bothered she was at that exact moment. She didn't want Eve to know that she'd just spent an hour in the ladies' room before approaching her. *Find your center, Anne,* she thought to herself. She imagined the peaceful commercial with the woman sitting in the bubble bath. Then she let her mind wander to holding Eve's head under the bubbles until she quit thrashing. While workplace violence never solved anything, Anne found the brief daydream somewhat soothing.

"Anne, you wanted to ask me something?" Eve brought Anne back to reality with a resounding crash.

"Um, yes, at my last performance appraisal, we had agreed on some action steps that I could work on that would help me earn this promotion." Anne kept her words steady and paced, attempting to hold the bubble thrashing daydream at bay … at least for the moment. "I worked very hard at achieving each one, and so I'm a little confused about why I was not on the promotion list this time."

There, she said it. Without crying, without raising her voice, very objectively and calmly, she said it.

"Well, Anne," Eve began her rehearsed spiel, "we did just say that working on these things would help you earn the promotion. We never did promise assurances now, did we?"

"Yes, but—" Anne could feel the color beginning to rise in her cheeks as Eve's so-called explanation continued to drown out her attempted interruption.

"You have indeed shown some marginal progress in these areas, Anne," the blood-red lipstick-lined mouth continued droning excuses. "But alas, 'marginal progress' isn't enough to earn a promotion. You really need to demonstrate mastery in these skills." Eve punctuated the comment with an obviously forced sigh.

"Mastery?" shot back Anne. "I've trained the last six people in the department who have all been promoted ahead of me. If that isn't showing mastery, I don't know what is."

"Oh now, Anne, let's not be bitter." Eve had the innate ability to choose the right tone to achieve the emotional equivalent of fingernails on a chalkboard. "Certainly, there is technical mastery in the job, which you have demonstrated almost admirably. Yet you lack some of the intangibles—those little *je ne sais quoi* that really separate the wheat from the chaff."

"Intangibles? Such as?" Anne was feeling the emotion creeping back into her voice. She knew this conversation was headed down the same road that many of the others had gone down in the past.

Why have the office hierarchy gods frowned on me so much? Anne wondered, internally bemoaning her plight of being stuck with this shark in red lipstick. Eve had a reputation for moving up the ladder by stepping on the backs of others. Many employees had left **REV**:Elation suddenly after crossing her path. Anne knew she must keep her cool if she wanted to keep her job.

"Well, your communication leaves a little to be desired. You're a little rough around the edges yet," the words oozed out of Eve's mouth like toxic sludge out of a barrel.

"Communication skills? So our CEO was lying to me last month when he wrote that note congratulating me on my presentation summarizing our project and saying how well I had facilitated the executive group through the question-and-answer session?"

"Now, now, Anne, we can't base an entire skill set on the basis of one little instance, can we? Otherwise, it would be easy for *everybody* to earn a promotion. Why don't we schedule some time to meet in a couple of weeks when you've had a chance to calm down? Perhaps I can counsel you through a few of these intangibles?" Eve batted her mascara-laden eyelashes purely for effect.

Anne had visions of the climactic scene from *The Wizard of Oz* in which Dorothy dumped the bucket of water on the Wicked Witch of the West. In the back of her mind, Anne wished she could hear Eve moaning, "I'm melting…" In reality, she mumbled a feeble agreement to the offer and mentioned something about needing to hurry to get to a meeting with her new project manager.

It was not turning out to be a pleasant day.

• • •

All the bases are loaded, thought Josh Matthews. I'm going for the grand slam home run.

For months, Josh had been working on the technical documentation for the project. He had worked closely with Vic, documenting every aspect of the product's design and specifications. Because all of this was critical before the formal public product launch, he had left no stone unturned. Vic's departure had upset Josh, but he knew he had to press forward and make sure all the key points were addressed. Now, all he needed was the team's approval and he would be able to meet this critical milestone. He wanted to be able to report success when meeting his new project manager for the first time.

He wrapped up his final presentation for his team. All of these people had a vested interest in making sure the product launch went well, and everyone around the table understood the critical role that this documentation played in making that happen. He was preparing for the question-and-answer period when Rani Blackburg eased herself (albeit less than graciously) into a chair by the door.

A few of the team members threw out various questions, mostly asking for simple clarifications that Josh provided easily. Heads were nodding all around the room—except one.

"Josh, I have a question."

"Yes, Rani?"

"Have you run all of this by the Legal Department for their approval?"

"Yes, Rani. I have." Ball one.

"Has Skip in Shipping seen this yet?"

Here it comes, he thought. *The onslaught of questions. She's going to make me experience death by inquisition.*

"Skip has not been identified as a stakeholder on this project. Skip's boss, Randall, has seen it, though, and is willing to take accountability for the entire Transportation division. I have his signature on the approval sheet already." Ball two.

So far, so good. Maybe she'll quit asking questions now.

"Has your new project manager viewed this information yet? I'm sure she probably has some insights into her own project."

"Since you brought it up, Rani, I have a meeting scheduled with her at three o'clock today. The whole team will be meeting her. I thought I would discuss it with her yet today so she could begin familiarizing herself with the project. I planned on getting her signature before I left the office."

"Well, I would not want to approve this until she had given

her nod to it."

Strike one. Rani continued.

"You know, while we're at it, I think that Dirk Runnells should look this over. After all, he is very thorough. I've been consulting for him for years, and I would trust his opinion."

Strike two. Things were looking less cheerful for Josh.

"Josh, why don't you obtain written signatures from the people I've mentioned in here today, and then you can schedule another meeting in a couple of weeks to get our approvals?"

"Because, Rani, I've had *this* meeting scheduled for weeks. The people in this room are difficult enough to get together as it is. This meeting was scheduled to obtain approvals. If you had other people you wanted on the approvals list, why didn't you bring them up weeks ago? Scheduling another meeting like this will set this part of the schedule back at least two months."

Rani smiled sweetly and innocently back at him, attempting to look sympathetic to his plight and ignoring the exasperated expressions of others in the room.

"You *seem* like a motivated guy, Josh, I'm sure you can do what's right so we don't have to elevate this to Dirk or even to Frank. Be a good boy and get the approvals I've asked for. Then we'll come back and vote again. I've got to run. Ta!" Condescension was Rani's specialty.

Strike three. Game over.

And with that, Rani Blackburg was gone as quickly as she had arrived. Also quickly gone were Josh's chances of getting approval on the technical documentation for the project.

I hope our new project manager likes to get nothing done, Josh thought. *Because that's exactly how much will be completed on the project she's inheriting.*

• • •

Isabella Gonzalez was a go-to person, a utility player. She was very good at getting done what needed to get done, even if she had to do it herself. Right now, she needed to obtain a couple of people for her project team from Michael Vanderpol, the manager of the Marketing department.

After numerous failed attempts to get an answer from Michael through email and phone, Isabella decided a face-to-face visit was necessary. Michael was known for acting somewhat scattered, which many suspected he used to his advantage when he didn't want to do something.

"Hi Michael," Isabella popped her head into his office quickly enough that he couldn't find a way to escape.

"Oh, Isabella, hi there, didn't expect to see you today," Michael said, looking a little befuddled, and Isabella surmised it was one of the first honest statements he had made to her.

"Well, Michael, you should know why I'm here. Have you identified the two people from your department that you will be assigning to our project?"

"Was that this week, already? Wow—time flies when you're having fun." Michael's feeble attempt to lighten the mood wasn't working.

"Oh, we're having fun? I wouldn't have noticed through all of the waiting. And actually, three weeks ago was the original deadline I needed you to identify the people for me. You do realize we're trying to work on the marketing and advertising information for the company's biggest product launch this year, don't you?" Isabella tried to keep her frustration in check.

"Well, we've been busy here. We don't just hand out marketing staff like candy. We need to think through who is available and who would be the right person for your needs," Michael replied, sounding mildly defensive to Isabella's comments.

"Michael, you've had the request for two months. It's been approved up and down the food chain. I've provided you with the exact skills I need from your staff as well as exactly what each one will be doing while on this project. I've emailed you. I've called you. I've provided you with documents, presentations, and spreadsheets. I've done everything except present my needs to you in the form of interpretive dance. There's no reason why you can't provide me with the names of two people." Isabella's patience with the situation had run out.

"You could do an interpretive dance to request resources? I'd love to see that," Michael said, clearly missing the point.

"How about this, Michael—you give me names now or I march into Frank Truman's office and tell him that you're slowing down this project. Which will it be?"

At this, Michael just laughed. "Like Frank Truman is going to do anything about it. He never dirties his hands at our level, and everybody here knows it. He's allergic to the details of the working class ilk. 'That's operations stuff. I'm all about strategy.'" Michael seemed to enjoy mimicking his CEO's well-worn line.

Isabella was shot down on that front. Still, she needed resources or once again she was going to have to do all the work herself. Michael's stonewalling was increasing her stress level.

"Look, Isabella, come back next month. I'll see what I can scrounge up for you around here. I just don't have time to deal with you right now."

Isabella could see her own workload growing exponentially if she were unable to get some assistance soon. This could be a very long product launch. And certainly was shaping up to be a very long day.

It's one thing to be a go-to person, she thought, *but to be a dumping ground is less than desirable.* Now she would have to explain the delay to her new project manager. At best, Vic was tolerant of delays; why should the new project manager be any better?

It was almost 3:00 as she made her way to the East Conference Room. Curiosity propelled her to find out what her new project manager would be like … and how much more work Isabella would have to do because of her.

• • •

> Hi Shay,
>
>> Any idea when the laptops will
>> be available? We'd really like to
>> get started on our work.

Shay Pradhan stared incredulously at the note left on his desk. It had been two weeks since he brought a team of ten rather expensive contractors on staff. They still didn't have computers to work on—no access to the network, no ability to send or receive emails. The productivity of the project was hampered. The cost of the project was skyrocketing.

Shay sighed as he picked up the phone. Calling Laurie Traiger was never a favorite activity of his—in fact it fell somewhere between dental work and cleaning the toilet. He had no idea how she ever landed the role of Help Desk manager as she was never helpful nor was she ever at her desk. On this day, however, he at least lucked out on the latter. The nasally voice blurted an impatient greeting on the other end of the line.

"Hi Laurie, any idea on the location of the laptops that I requested a month ago?" Shay just wanted to get work done. He stayed objective and got right to the issue. He never liked to take sides or get involved in conflict. Staying neutral and getting past roadblocks was all he cared about.

"Shay, I've told you the last five times you called that these things need to go through channels. How hard is that for you to understand?"

"It's only hard to understand that the amount I've lost in

labor cost from my computerless consultants is more than the fully loaded laptops would cost. Would it be easier if I just went to the closest Compu-Buy Store and purchased the laptops myself?" Shay suppressed the frustration in his voice to offer the best solution he could think of to allow progress to return to his project.

"Shay, you realize that it is against **REV**:Elation policy for employees to purchase their own computer equipment. All requisitions must be processed through the Help Desk," Laurie droned the policy from memory; it wasn't the first time she had heard this suggestion.

"Laurie, I understand what company policy is and why it exists. What I don't understand is why your department is taking weeks to perform a task that I could do myself in a couple of hours." The irritation was seeping into Shay's voice. "By the way, Laurie, you wouldn't happen to have any kind of status that would tell me where my order is and when it will be fulfilled, would you?"

"Are you questioning my department's ability to fulfill your order, Shay?" The defensiveness was obvious.

"Not in the least, Laurie. As a matter of fact, I'm quite certain you've either lost or 'accidentally' erased the requisition. Meanwhile, I'm losing thousands of dollars each day in productivity because of it!" Shay's patience had run out. "Look, I realize that you are distracted by many other priorities; however, I need to provide my team with the right equipment, not babysit your department through a simple purchase order."

"Talking to me like that is both unwelcomed and unappreciated," Laurie said, her generally cordial demeanor becoming more acidic with every word.

So I've been hired to cure your bad case of managerial disorganization, Shay thought. *After I do that, I'll create world peace and find a universal cure for global disease.*

"Why don't you resubmit your requisition and we'll see what we can do?" continued Laurie. "Perhaps I can make things go a little more smoothly the second time."

"A second time, eh?" Shay resolved himself to the inevitable. "OK, if that's what it will take. But I want to know something, Laurie: When will this company start putting commonsense over company policy? And who's going to subsidize the additional lost productivity of my team while this order is being lost … er, I mean, processed?"

"If you would like to escalate this issue, I can provide you with the necessary paperwork to file a complaint," Laurie replied icily.

"No thanks, Laurie. First, I have to go to a meeting with my new project manager. Second, I'd like this issue resolved before I retire in thirty years."

Shay hung up the phone, wondering where his normally neutral approach to handling conflict had gone wrong. He looked at his watch. He'd have just enough time to go meet the newest project manager hired at *REV*:Elation. He wasn't sure why they hired an outsider instead of promoting somebody already on the project. Either way, he was going to have to explain why he was burning through his share of the budget with nothing to show for it. The day kept getting worse.

Chapter 4

Liz watched and waited as her team slowly and sporadically filed into the East Conference Room for the introductory meeting she had scheduled. None of the individuals looked especially excited to meet her, but to Liz, it didn't appear that she was the cause of their apathetic demeanor. Frank had warned her that there may be some fallout for hiring an outsider rather than promoting from within; however, from Liz's perspective, each one of the team members was preoccupied with something other than getting to know the new project manager. Given what she had already observed during her first few hours at *REV*:Elation, Liz had her suspicions for the general bad mood.

"I'm Liz Meredith, Vic Elliott's replacement," she said, and so began the obligatory introductions. Because she still had to protect her professional identity and reputation beyond this project, Liz chose to speak of her experience in somewhat general terms. When the team would push for more details, Liz would provide as much information as she perceived was relevant; however, her new staff only occasionally tested the boundaries of how much information they asked.

While she talked, she spent time watching each of her team

members and attempting to make eye contact with all of them. Liz felt that she could get a better read on each person through body language and facial expressions. The cold, blank stares on many of their faces became unsettling after about the first fifteen minutes. Introductions were curt, and status reports were very formal. This behavior from the team continued throughout the first meeting. The second and third meetings spanning the next few days were not much of an improvement over the first. Communication was terse, and conversations stayed on a superficial level, at least when she was anywhere within earshot.

The evening before their fourth status meeting, Liz reflected on her team's behavior. They were obviously gun-shy and didn't trust outsiders. If what Frank had told her about the state of office politics was true, then their behaviors were understandable and predictable. Still, she had to find a way to ease her team into a conversation where they would feel comfortable opening up to her. She decided that she would have to try a slightly more direct approach.

"Alright, I'll bite," Liz began when this status meeting started the same way as the others. "I know we haven't known each other long, but you all could stand to give a better first impression."

"Sorry we didn't roll out the red carpet," Dee Connors offered in the way of a sarcastic apology. "We didn't realize the world needed to stop for your arrival."

"Don't mind Dee," interrupted Josh Matthews. "She's just bitter about being one-upped by Mark Washington again."

"Yes, Josh, I am," shot back Dee. "And tell me, how's your backside after your latest phone lashing from Dirk Runnells? I hear he added more cell minutes to his plan just to yell at you on a regular basis."

"That must have been Dirk who was on the elevator with me the first day," Liz observed wryly. Then, hoping to deflect the obvious tension growing quickly between Josh and Dee, she continued with a grin. "I had the—ahem—pleasure of listening to one of his mobile lashings. Sorry you have to endure those. It was pretty harsh from where I was standing."

"Dirk is in a perpetually bad mood," Isabella Gonzalez spoke up. "I'm guessing there's not enough fiber in his diet," she added in the way of attempted humor.

"So, Isabella, how are things going with Michael Vanderpol?" Josh asked earnestly. "Has he agreed to give us more resources to complete the marketing plan?"

"He's agreed to more resources in the same way that Rani Blackburg has agreed to approve your technical documents," laughed Isabella halfheartedly. Obviously, the two had debriefed on their respective problems before.

"Don't tell me you two are still having problems?" groaned Anne Ericsen with a sigh. "I can't believe all the political problems this project gets into."

"It hits us all, Anne," added Shay Pradhan, knowing where she was coming from. "I think I speak for all of us when I say I'm sorry your name wasn't on the promotion list this quarter. Nobody on this team has worked harder to earn it."

"Well, Eve and I did have a chat when the list came out, and she did say there are things I still need to work on," Anne said rather matter-of-factly to the eye-rolling of certain team members. "It will happen."

"Not until you return her ruby slippers," cackled Dee, and then added with a sly smile, "… and your little dog, too!"

The whole team chuckled at *The Wizard of Oz* reference since they all had supported Anne through her challenges with Eve. Additionally, they were perplexed about what was fueling those challenges. It appeared to Liz as though the comment about *The Wizard of Oz* had broken the ice a little … or at least cracked it. The comfort level had increased enough to begin the work for which she was really hired.

"I see we've hit on a common thread," Liz allowed herself to laugh with the team at the current state of affairs. "Does everyone in this room feel that office politics are a problem around here?"

Emphatic nods of agreement came from her team. Slowly,

they opened up and began sharing stories going back years. The evidence of a political culture was mounting. At some points in the conversation, it almost grew to a frenzy of one-upping each other on how bad certain departments or individuals were. Everybody had horror stories to bring to the table. And Liz—at least mentally—was taking notes.

Liz waited until the banter began to die down for the opportune moment to make her offer.

"I can relate to what all of you are talking about," Liz confessed. "I've been bitten by office politics more times than I care to admit. I've just learned to deal with it over the years."

"Deal with it?" Dee challenged. "You make it sound like a broken fingernail or a snag in your hose. So, exactly what does one do to 'deal with it'?"

"Jeez, Dee, don't you ever back off?" Shay was appalled at his colleague's abrasive behavior as he glanced apologetically at Liz. "Did you ever think that somebody *outside* of **REV**:Elation might know a trick or two that we don't?"

"Thank you, Shay," Liz acknowledged, "but I'd say that Dee has a right to feel how she does about politics. However, I have learned a few tricks in that area over the years. Would you all be interested in a little coaching to help you identify and handle office politics more effectively?"

"You and what army?" countered Dee. Clearly, throughout the dialogue thus far, Dee was the most overtly bitter and defensive.

"Just us. We're all in this together," shot back Liz without missing a beat.

"It just seems, Liz, that political tactics in this company are always shifting," complained Josh. "Whenever I think I have a handle on who has what issues with what department or what person, it all changes."

"He's right, but I still don't think I want any part of it," Anne said. "The way people treat each other around here is deplorable. They're all just out to get something and then it's like wind shifting on the sand ... they're off to nail somebody else."

"You know, Anne, you may not like office politics, but you just made a very astute observation, and provided me with an effective transition to share with you an approach for how you can deal with them," Liz continued despite Anne's puzzled look. "Politics *are* like the wind in many respects. You can't see either one directly, but you can see and feel the effects of both. Both can range in force from a light breeze that can help alleviate an unpleasant situation to a fierce tornado that can cause a lot of damage."

"Cute metaphor," stated Shay, his interest piqued. "Do you have any substance to back it up?"

In answer to his commentary, Liz walked over to the flip chart easel and wrote the following:

Office Politics 101
Game
U
S
T

"GUST?" he responded in a deadpan voice. "Wow, just what our company needs, another acronym."

"Bear with me," Liz replied. "I promised to help you all survive your political battles. GUST is the process by which we'll do that. And we'll start with the **Game**."

"Game?" quizzed Isabella. "Since when is the problem of office politics a game? I never feel like I'm having fun when I'm stuck playing politics."

"Or when the game is being played on me," interjected Josh.

Liz turned around and faced her team to explain. "Most of office politics is a game ... at least to somebody. Keep in mind, too, that when I talk about a game, I'm not limiting the term simply to children's playtime. Complex strategies use gaming theories to test the validity of an approach. Simulation is also a type of game, constantly playing 'what if' scenarios to determine what could happen under different circumstances. I would encourage you all to broaden your definitions of the word."

"Fair enough," replied Isabella skeptically. "But I go back to my original question: What relevance do games have with respect to office politics?"

"Let me answer your question with a question: When do you realize that you're a victim of politics?" Liz never missed a chance at a teachable moment.

"Usually when it's all over but the crying," Isabella admitted to her new project manager.

"That's true," Anne piped up. "I usually never know that politics are going on around me until things blow up in my face. Of course, I don't even like to think that people act that way, but I'm sure that the signs were probably there all along … like with Eve."

"Anne, for somebody who claims to hate politics as much as you do, you sure have a knack for putting your finger right on the pulse of the issue," Liz praised, to Anne's embarrassment. "You're correct. Even though the signs and evidence of politics are present, most of us don't realize the games that are being played against us, even though we may be the one who inadvertently started the game in play."

"How so?" Anne was becoming more intrigued with each moment.

"Think about all of the stories all of you shared just now. Each of you had requested something, let somebody else know you needed something, or complained because you didn't have something. That set the game in motion for the other party. It's the equivalent of throwing out the first pitch. The other party had the choice of whether or not they wanted to swing at that pitch." Liz could tell the team was starting to pay attention. She continued with the explanation.

"It's important with almost any face-to-face exchange— especially one where the people involved don't know or trust each other very well—to consider the effects of what you're asking, requesting, demanding, or telling. Each request, each requisition, each phone call, or each email may be the beginning of another game. Often, we don't even think before we ask for something. After all, each game is different."

"What do you mean by that?" Shay looked almost panicked. "Are you telling us that we need to be concerned not only about politics but also the kinds of politics that are being played?"

"Of course, Shay," Liz paced herself. "Going back to our ball game example, if you asked somebody to play ball with you, wouldn't you specify with them what kind of ball game you were playing? You wouldn't want to show up with a baseball bat and your friend with a football, would you?"

"No," came the mumbled answer to the obvious.

"Every political game, just like every ball game, comes down to manipulation of some kind," Liz continued. "You just have to figure out what type of manipulation is occurring. You must identify your game ball. Applying it to our situation, people playing the political game are either manipulating resources, information, or people."

"Can you be a little more specific?" Dee was skeptical, but was showing some signs of opening up. "That sounds a little academic."

Liz smiled. "Yes, Dee, consider this. You asked Mark for some facts and figures from an executive retreat that he didn't want to share. That's an example of withholding information. He outright refused, but sometimes the manipulation is more subtle and covert. Sometimes people will provide incorrect information, or be overly literal in the information provided. With Mark, withholding information was a way of maintaining control. The fact remains, however, that you started the game in motion by making the request in the first place."

"I think I was a victim of incorrect information," observed Shay, shifting to his own experience. "Laurie Traiger uses smoke and mirrors to cover her inability to get things done in her department. When asked directly, she couldn't provide an objective status on my laptop order. Instead, she tried to hide behind company policy to cover her tracks. So, in a sense, she's manipulating information using misinformation, right?"

"Very good example," confirmed Liz. "And the resources manipulation game has some of the same characteristics as the information game. It focuses on hoarding, hiding, changing, switching, or otherwise playing with things like time, money, organizational structures, systems, or other territorial ground."

"But what about my situation?" threw in Isabella. "I want people, but those people are also resources to our project. So which is it?"

"Ah, we Western thinkers," Liz said with a smile. She'd been down this road before. "Everything has to fit tidily into only one category. What's to say, Isabella, that your situation doesn't fall into both? The people manipulation game deals with relationships, control, balance of power, communication, or anything that impacts how people interact, to whom they report, or what they perceive. So, in short, there are no simple lines we can draw in every situation. It sounds like yours may fall into both. Just like Dee's could be both information and resources."

"So I'm guessing my manipulation game may fall into all three," Josh piped in. "I need approvals on a document to move forward. The approvals in and of themselves may be resources, but Rani keeps muddying the waters with additional information and layers of approvals, and she's using her relationships to control who approves them and when—all to slow the process down."

"Trust me, Josh, nobody understands more about slowing things down through manipulation than I do," moped Anne. "I've been bucking for the promotion for months, and Eve appears to be the only thing standing between it and me. The operative question I have isn't what the game is, but why is she playing this game with me?"

"Once again, Anne, your intuition for guiding the

conversation is uncanny," Liz said. "That's what we're going to cover in our next meeting. Until then, I want you all to examine some of your political conflicts, and see if you can identify what kinds of games are being played. This step is very important because if you can recognize that a game is being played, as well as identify the type of game that is being played, that means you are becoming aware of the office politics being played around you. Once you've mastered this, then we'll begin to talk about why these games are being played."

The meeting ended with small talk among the team, but now Liz was included in the conversation. As the team departed, their curiosity about their new project manager had increased. Each of them wondered about the assistance she would provide them in dealing with their greatest political challenges.

Chapter 5

Liz continued following the same path she would if she were serving in her regular corporate capacity as an investigator: absorbing and learning as much about her project and about *REV*:Elation's organizational structure and political relationships as she could. She learned that Dirk Runnells, the Chief Operating Officer, had quite a reputation for bullying everybody in the organization. That certainly aligned with the behavior she observed in the elevator on her first day. For some reason, Frank had neglected to provide any relevant level of detail about Dirk's role and his reputation, given his presence and importance within the organization. Liz also spent some time quietly and covertly observing her team members as well as those who were challenging them in various ways. Because each of her team's antagonists maintained a fairly high profile in the organization, watching their behaviors firsthand was not difficult.

Although Liz did not have direct authority over her project team members, she made it clear to each of them that she would maintain an open door policy. Many of them came to her throughout the week for clarification on various things regarding the product launch, but little was mentioned about office politics or GUST until their next scheduled status meeting.

The day of the team meeting, Isabella and Dee decided to meet for lunch in the company cafeteria. Upon entering, they noticed Anne sitting at a table in the furthest corner, away from the crowds. As they approached her, it became evident that Anne had experienced another run-in with Eve.

"Uh-oh. Looks like somebody got nailed again," Dee said, noticing Anne's tear-stained face. "How bad was it this time?"

"I don't want to talk about it," came Anne's muffled reply.

"You can't keep letting her push you around, Anne," Isabella offered supportively. "She's making you miserable. Can't you transfer to a different department or go to HR?"

The suggestions only upset Anne more. "I've tried to get a transfer, but she's ruined it every time. She either puts damaging things in my employee file, or she tells the manager in the other department that she 'simply can't part with my skills and abilities right now.'"

"And as far as HR goes, they are neither human, nor are they a resource," Dee interrupted, to Anne's agreement. Human Resources at *REV*:Elation was infamous for its reputation as policy police and nothing more; they simply existed to ensure rules were followed.

"Have you talked to Liz about this yet?" Isabella was not about to give up. Normally, she would have just listened empathetically to her colleague's problems as a show of support, but the time for passive help was over. Anne needed solutions. This situation had been going on for months.

"How do I know she's not just another manager out to screw me over?" queried Anne.

"Anne, you're the last person any of us would expect to become cynical," countered Dee, surprised at the response they received. "Besides, that's my job," she added with a smile.

"Dee is right. You are too talented and too nice of a person to let this problem hold you back, let alone turn you bitter." Isabella was becoming alarmed that her friend was affected to this degree by her problem. "Why don't you bring it up this afternoon at the meeting? We'll stand beside you. You may have to fight fire with fire."

"I could never stoop to playing politics," Anne protested adamantly. "It's not ethical. It's not moral. I'll have nothing to do with it!" She softened a little and added, "But I will bring it up with Liz this afternoon. Thanks for sticking by me."

The remainder of the afternoon went quickly. Anne, not wanting to engage in the perceived messiness of office politics, was extremely hesitant at the thought of even participating in a conversation on the topic. Still, the prospect of help appeared promising, if remote. What did she have to lose?

The team showed up promptly to the meeting this week. They quickly went through the standard project updates, this time faster than normal. Liz then entered the next phase of politics conversation by asking them if they had had a chance to think about her challenge from the previous week. She was pleasantly surprised that in only a few days they were feeling open enough to share details about their real political games involving the manipulation of resources, information, and people. She was also alarmed by the number and severity of the examples they mentioned. They built upon many of the observations they had shared at the last meeting. The general conclusion was that most political games involved a combination of two or all three types of manipulation; rarely was the game isolated to a single facet, although one of the three generally emerged as the prevalent factor. They also shared that they were able to isolate what the "game ball" was, either through follow-up conversations with the individuals with whom they were experiencing conflict, or by watching body language and vocal tone in meetings. Finding hot buttons was never hard, and it became pretty obvious when a sensitive request was being made or followed up on.

The team showed great adeptness at understanding the subtleties of these manipulations, and some of their examples showed that they grasped the complexities of different kinds of games. Often, they had the look of relief akin to what an ill patient expresses when a doctor is able to diagnose the illness. They were beginning to comprehend how the simplest of exchanges and transactions was triggering some of their most frustrating political battles.

"Well, at least I'm glad you are all able to identify some of the games being played. As we talked about last week, identifying the point of manipulation is the first tool you have in battling politics," Liz tried to sound positive, but inside she was concerned about the degree to which office politics were being played at *REV*:Elation.

"Yes, I think we get the whole 'game' concept, Liz," interjected Josh. "But I'm more concerned about knowing why the game is being played."

"I agree," added Anne. "I still hate the idea of politics altogether, and I'd rather not get involved. But at least if I understand why other people are playing them, it may help me avoid them more."

"Well, Anne, I won't promise to help you avoid politics," answered Liz. "But the next stage in harnessing the shifting winds of corporate politics involves **Understanding**." With that, Liz referred to the flip chart sheet she had started the week prior:

Office Politics 101
Game
Understand
S
T

"Understand what?" asked Isabella.
"Understand who?" questioned Dee.
"Understand how?" inquired Shay.
"Understand why?" added Anne.
"All of the above," Liz answered quickly. "Understanding

involves looking at all angles of the game. What is really going on? Who are the real players involved? Why are they doing what they are doing? What is motivating the resulting behaviors?"

"But how are we supposed to find out what is behind their motives?" pressed Anne.

"Yeah," interjected Dee, shifting into her trademark sarcastic tone. "Do we simply go up and ask, 'Excuse me, can you please tell me why you're being nominated as the dysfunctional poster child?'"

"If it were that simple," responded Liz amid the team's snickering, "would you really even need me—or any manager, for that matter—around to help you? Part of understanding is simply asking some questions when it becomes evident that a political game is being played. Sometimes you'll ask questions directly to the person you're having the conflict with. Other times, you may be asking those who are involved through some minor role or who are simply observing."

"What kind of questions would we ask?" countered Shay, then he added with a grin, "Dee's response seems a little too direct."

"The trick is to ask questions that will eventually get to the heart of the behavior being observed and the game that you think is being played. You have to be able to play detective during this phase of solving office politics. Dee, let's take your situation with Mark Washington as an example."

Dee looked at her project manager with skepticism. "Must we?"

"Actually, yes," directed Liz. "Because I want the information in the report that he's withholding as badly as you do, and I really don't want to have to leverage Frank Truman to solve our problems any more than necessary."

"OK," responded Dee, in a challenging tone that made it clear to Liz she was going to have to prove herself.

"Why would Mark withhold that information? What would motivate him to be less than cooperative?"

"Outside of a generally unpleasant personality?" countered Dee.

"Dee, tone it down; she's trying to help us," reprimanded Isabella, then turned to Liz. "To answer your question, Mark likes the feeling of power he gets when he can hold something over somebody's head. It's not just this information; he's very territorial with everything. He maintains his department like it's some kind of cult; all information has to flow through him or he blows a gasket. My department interacts with his on a regular basis."

"Dee, is that how you perceive the situation?" asked Liz, not wanting to leave Dee out of the conversation.

"I guess so," Dee responded in a more humble and accepting tone after being scolded by her peer. "He likes to think that he's more powerful than he really is. He hates change, because he feels it threatens his power, so he always fights to keep things just the way they are. He also doesn't like anything that will make his life more challenging, or add work to his department."

"Now we're getting somewhere!" Liz was becoming more enthusiastic. "Generally speaking, the understanding phase of managing politics boils down to one primary thing: motivation."

"Like what?" asked Josh. "There are a lot of directions you can go with simply blaming politics on motivations. That seems a bit theoretical."

"Keep in mind," Liz reminded the group as she walked to the flip chart easel, "that all of politics starts with a game to manipulate something."

"Resources, information, or people," interjected Anne.

"Exactly," Liz responded. "But it's not enough to know what is being manipulated. When you're embroiled in politics, you also have to figure out *why* the person playing the game is manipulating the resources, information, and/or people."

"That could be just about anything, though," groaned Josh. "I've known managers around here to be difficult because they have a hangnail or because their spouse talked to them the wrong way that morning."

"Perhaps that was a catalyst to spur the behavior," observed

Liz, "but it probably wasn't the sole motivator. Generally, people are motivated to play political games by six different factors." And with that, she approached the flipchart and drew a diagram:

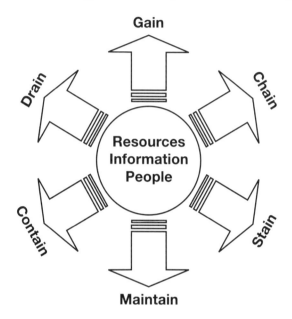

"The **gain** motivation should be pretty self-explanatory," began Liz. "Politicians sometimes want something they don't already have, so they will attempt to gain it."

"Like my self-esteem," whispered Anne to Isabella, thinking painfully of her many exchanges with Eve.

"So, if a manager were trying to get another department reporting to him or her, that would be an example of gaining?" Josh clarified.

"Right," Liz continued. "Next, to **chain** something is to pull together two or more things into a relationship that didn't exist before. I tend to see this in people, when they build alliances with others they don't necessarily like."

"Well, they say that politics do make strange bedfellows,"

offered Josh, to the agreement of the others in the room.

"Exactly, Josh," confirmed Liz. "And that reminds me: Do you know why Rani Blackburg is continually stalling approval for your product documentation?"

"Other than just being mean-spirited, I'm not really sure," admitted Josh.

"You had mentioned that she often uses her business relationship with Dirk Runnells to hold things up. Do you realize that Rani's husband and Dirk served together in the military? Rani and Dirk have known each other for years. Dirk got Rani the consulting contract at *REV*:Elation, and our project threatens Rani's long-term contract here. In addition, Rani has been building an alliance with Dirk for months because she would like to become his 'second in command.' And all of that means that the 'chain' of their relationship is motivating Rani to want to 'stain' our project."

"How did you find all that out?" asked Josh incredulously.

"It's amazing what one finds out when working out in the fitness center," Liz responded nonchalantly with an ever-so-slight grin.

"But what do you mean by staining our project?" Shay got back on track and looked inquisitively at Liz, who was now pointing at the next motivator on the chart.

"To **stain** is essentially to ruin something, stop it, or destroy it. It may be done through a tactic as obvious as sabotage or undermining, or it may be veiled in innuendo and guessing— attacking the reputation rather than the thing or person itself. There are as many ways to ruin initiatives in companies as there are initiatives themselves. I'm guessing that Rani thinks that by stalling parts of our project, she can stain it enough to get it canceled so she can continue working at *REV*:Elation and so she can improve her standing with Dirk."

"She can't do that!" protested Josh. "So, how did you find this out? Did you just walk up to her during your morning workout and ask her why she was making my life miserable?"

"Hardly, Josh. It was as simple as listening and observing," came Liz's response. "It's something you all should be doing every day. Unfortunately, we get so caught up in our own day-to-day problems that we forget to pay attention to everyone and everything around us. And the answers generally are there waiting to be found if we look."

"What do you mean?" probed Anne. "How do we uncover the answers?"

"It's not really that complicated, Anne," Liz knew she had struck a nerve. "As we talked about earlier, it can be as simple as watching people's body language in a meeting. Try striking up a conversation at the water cooler. Sit at the table beside your adversaries in the cafeteria, preferably not letting them notice you are there. Look at how people decorate their offices with personal effects. Often people are careless about their conversations. If they don't keep private conversations behind closed doors then you may be in a position to overhear their careless banter. Spend a couple of extra minutes in a restroom stall. Casually listen in on a cell phone conversation if the person is loud enough and careless enough to let you hear. Put yourself in a position to observe and listen to people. All of these behaviors speak volumes about others' values, personalities, and motivations. Your eyes and ears are your chief input devices, but many of us neglect to use them regularly." Liz knew she had made her point, so she decided to get back on track with Dee's conflict with Mark.

"Dee, knowing what we now know about Mark Washington and what appears to be motivating him, what category or categories of motivation would you use to describe your political conflict?" Dee shifted uncomfortably at Liz's directness, but Liz could tell that she had Dee's attention.

"Well …" began Dee, "I'm guessing that **maintain** is probably a big part of it, since he never wants anything to change that would negatively affect him. Any change is met with immediate resistance from him or his henchmen, so he really likes to maintain the status quo. Am I on the right track?"

"Perfectly," affirmed Liz. "Anything else?"

"Since he's always trying to keep or build his power base by hoarding information and preventing his people from leaving the department, another of his motivators is most likely to **contain** things. Employees are always calling him a departmental black hole since people and information go in, but they never come out." The others grinned at Dee's comparison.

"Excellent, Dee," encouraged Liz. "Now, how could knowing these motivators be useful in helping you deal more effectively with Mark?"

"Well, I probably shouldn't insult him constantly," admitted Dee, then turning suddenly defensive. "He just always knows what buttons to push to really irritate me. I can't help myself."

"We'll work on that," promised Liz calmly. "Shay, you have a question?"

"Well, yes," he piped up after a period of silence. "What about that last one. What does it mean to **drain**?"

"Draining is the opposite of gaining. Simply put, you are trying to take something away. Unlike staining, you may not be trying to destroy it altogether; you merely want it diminished or removed in some way."

"So when Laurie Traiger is so scattered that she can't focus, and she tries to blame mistakes on other people, she's merely trying to drain their credibility to cover her own incompetence?" Shay was sincere in his inquiry.

"Laurie has never been able to focus," Isabella interjected. "She and I used to be on the same team, and she was incapable of prioritizing back then. She was constantly overwhelmed by everything, bombarded by crises and changes and requests. Most of her problems she created herself by not giving them the attention they needed when she could have handled the problems more effectively."

"How on earth did she get promoted?" Shay quizzed Isabella incredulously.

"She was a hard worker and put in long hours, mostly because she created so much work for herself by her lack of organization. However, she was always able to deflect the blame for her shortcomings, so they promoted her." By Isabella's tone, it was obvious she was not impressed with management's decision to move Laurie up the ladder.

"OK, team, your assignment for next week," interrupted Liz, looking at the clock on the wall, "is to familiarize yourselves with the motivations behind the games that are being played. Again, the trick here is to watch and observe and learn. As always, come to me any time if you have questions."

Chapter 6

Anne was feeling very conflicted that evening. She had long held the belief that all office politics were bad and that the people who engaged in them were immoral and unethical. Anne's values stemmed from her conservative religious background, and she sometimes was perceived as being very dogmatic in her beliefs. More than one person at *REV*:Elation had made passing references to her occasional holier-than-thou approach to life, either seriously or in jest. Yet those who knew her well were aware of her unparalleled integrity.

Anne was still troubled as she went to her weekly church Bible study that evening. It was the group's last night studying the characters in the Old Testament and they learned about Nehemiah, the man who was responsible for rallying Israel to rebuild the wall around Jerusalem after the exiles began returning to their land. As Anne listened to the story of Nehemiah, she began to see parallels between what he was doing and the office politics she was learning about. Nehemiah was a close servant to a foreign king. He successfully persuaded the king to think it was his own idea to send Nehemiah back to his homeland, and he was able to convince the king to provide him with the resources he would need for a safe passage back to Jerusalem and to rebuild the wall once he arrived there. When he arrived in Israel, Nehemiah had to deal with people who did not want the wall rebuilt. They tried sabotaging his character, luring him into ambush, and distracting the other Israelites (who also fought amongst themselves) to prevent the wall from being rebuilt—yet he successfully led the rebuilding of the wall in less than two months.

As discussion wrapped up, Anne couldn't help asking the group: "So, based on what we read and talked about, would you say that Nehemiah was playing office politics?"

The responses varied from abject denial that a biblical character would engage in such activity to half-hearted acknowledgement that it seemed he was engaging in politics. Finally, a young woman named Grace spoke up.

"Anne, a lot of time our morals are called into action in very strange ways. On occasion, we have to go on the defensive. Other times, we have to consider the greater good that comes out of our less-than-perfect actions. Think about some of the other characters we've discussed. There was the woman who misled her own husband on purpose to ensure that her favorite son would receive the inheritance that should have belonged to his twin brother. Or the man whose brothers sold him into slavery during his boyhood out of jealousy and spite—when the power shifted and he became an Egyptian ruler, he played cloak and dagger with them and kept his identity secret until the time was right to reveal who he was."

Anne looked startled. She'd never put those characters in that kind of context. Grace kept going.

"We complain about our projects taking too long to get done, but how would you feel if you were Moses and your project took 40 years longer than planned because the people involved were easily distracted and loved to fight among themselves? Or think of Queen Esther, who risked her life by disobeying her husband in order to ultimately unmask his favored right-hand man as an underhanded villain.

"From the time Christ was born until now, not much has improved in the way we handle disagreements and conflicts. Jesus' close followers were always jockeying for position. After churches began to crop up, the politics just got more intense. The number of alliances made, lives lost, sides taken, and arguments started in the name of moral religious piety is enough to make your head spin. And each major religion has some degree of conflict built into its history and its present."

Anne sat in silence. Clearly she had not thought about all of the contexts of office politics. Even in her own church she saw some of the same behaviors that plagued her team at the office. The light bulb clicked on in Anne's head, and she wasn't sure how to react to it. She would have a long and sleepless night ahead of her.

Anne showed the effects of her lack of sleep the next day. Liz had called a sudden project team meeting to deal with a specific issue. The team handled the problem rather quickly and began to reopen the prior day's discussion about politics.

Liz could tell during the entire meeting that something was amiss with Anne. To Liz, Anne was a young woman who, despite her strongly voiced resistance to office politics, appeared to be very astute at observing and assessing the people and situations around her. She had a keen ability to size up her environment quickly and objectively, a trait Liz valued and admired because it was critical to her own career success. Liz was perplexed by what she had heard and observed about Eve's treatment of Anne. Although Eve tended to approach everybody with a certain degree of sadistic unpleasantness, Anne appeared to be her favorite target. While the others continued their conversation about the political motivations of their respective antagonists, Liz looked expectantly at Anne. Finally, the two made eye contact.

"What?" Anne asked, almost defensively.

"Nothing," Liz said, attempting an innocent look to coax Anne into the conversation. "You just looked like you had something on your mind."

"Something has been bothering me," admitted Anne.

"Is it Eve?" Liz asked, then almost kicked herself the moment the words left her mouth. Jumping the gun was not something she normally did.

"Actually, Eve is only part of the problem," admitted Anne. "I think I'm struggling with the whole concept of playing politics. I've always thought that playing office politics was so … so … evil."

Dee, in her normal abrasive style, piped up in agreement. "Anne is right, though. Most of the managers around *REV: Elation* are just dirty, rotten SOBs."

Anne looked up in alarmed protest at Dee's choice of terminology. "I would never use that term, Dee!" The rest of the team also appeared a little surprised at Dee's unprofessional word choice. Surprisingly, Liz jumped to Dee's defense.

"Anne, in a sense Dee is right, although I use SOB to stand for something a little gentler than what Dee is thinking of. When I hear people accusing office politicians of being SOBs, I classify all them as **Snakes**, **Ostriches**, or **Bears**."

"You've lost me," Anne said, staring blankly at her project manager.

"Snakes should be fairly obvious to you, since you're dealing with one right now, Anne," Isabella joined the conversation.

"That's right, Isabella," continued Liz. "A snake politician is the one we're all familiar with. He or she is the credit-stealer, the one who will stab you in the back, the employee who purposely keeps everybody off-guard, the person who only cares about getting ahead and what's in it for him or her, regardless of who gets hurt in the process. Morals and ethics mean nothing to this person."

"Sure sounds like Eve," Dee offered in support.

"However, not every politician is like that," countered Liz. "You all know what ostriches are famous for."

"Yes, they love to stick their head in the ground. The myth is that they are scared, but most likely they are searching for food or water," Shay said, enjoying the opportunity to contribute a piece to trivia.

"Regardless of why they do it, they still are avoiding what they can see above ground," countered Liz. "So it is with an ostrich politician. It may be ignorance or an avoidance strategy, but the fact remains: They're not engaging in what they see right in front of them."

"I guess that's how I've been behaving," Anne said, looking rather sheepish. "It's just that I was taught that there was good and bad, and that the behaviors that politicians engage in are bad."

Liz continued to the next logical step. "Anne, do you think it's ever possible for somebody to behave politically and ethically at the same time?"

"Before yesterday, I would have said no. Today, I'm not so sure. Ethics and morals can be subjective and relative at times, but I suppose it depends on the perceptions of those acting and those observing," Anne answered after thinking about the question for a few moments.

Liz was truly surprised that Anne appeared to be softening on the subject. She made a mental note to ask Anne later what had happened to shift her thinking. Anne looked back at Liz almost expectantly. Clearly, the rest of the team noticed the change in Anne's thinking, and they were amazed that she might finally admit that playing politics didn't mean an automatic pass to Hell.

"Is that where the bear politician comes into play?" Anne asked, finally breaking the long silence that followed her previous comment.

"You guessed it," answered Liz. "A bear in the wild generally does not attack unless provoked. It must feel that its livelihood is being threatened in some way. So it is with bear politicians. They aren't afraid to play political games, but they have a bigger picture in mind, something larger than their own goals and aspirations. They play politics for the good of the team, the project, or the organization. For them, politics is not about gaining personal influence; it's about accomplishing the goal. Bear politicians have a bigger vision in mind than simply acquiring power."

"OK, now you've opened a can of worms, Liz," Josh piped up. "How do people get the power to influence others in an organization?"

"Good question, Josh," Liz responded as she traveled back to her trusty flip chart. "During my career, I've noticed that influence has a RIPPLE effect. There are six sources by which people influence others, and that influence radiates to those who are impacted. Sometimes these are earned, other times they may be bestowed upon a person, and frequently they may be gained by less than honorable means. As with most of the issues we've talked about, none of them are inherently bad unless they're overused or taken to the extreme. A shrewd politician learns to use all of them appropriately, but only as needed."

Then Liz began to write:

The "Ripple Effect" of Influence
Reprimand
Incentive
Position
Personality
Liaison
Expert

"Oh no, not another acronym!" groaned Shay.

"Well, it *does* help to remember all of this information," defended Liz. "As I just said, influence and power have a 'RIPPLE' effect, which everyone should keep in mind when dealing with office politics. But let me ask you all, what do you think these mean?"

"The first two seem very obvious," Dee stated wryly. "Pretty much just punishment and reward, isn't it? Stick with me and nobody gets hurt?"

"Yes," Liz agreed, with a chuckle at Dee's comment. "The danger in these two comes from overuse. An inexperienced leader who gets a favorable response after one or two uses tends to fall into the habit of using them over and over again."

"But doesn't that tend to erode their credibility?" Josh added. "Didn't Abraham Maslow once say that if the only tool you have is a hammer then every problem looks like a nail?"

"Good application, Josh," affirmed Liz, "I've used that Maslow quote many times to get an idea across to a coworker. But you have a point. After a while, that person's professional reputation can be tied to the type of influence that he or she uses. And **reprimands** and **incentives** seem very easy to dole out, which is why many managers fall into the trap of overusing them."

"What do you mean by **position** as an influencer?" asked Anne.

"How many of you are parents?" Liz answered her question with a question, to which Dee, Josh, and Isabella raised their hands.

"Which of you three, when your requests or demands have been questioned by your children, have simply answered, 'Because I'm the mom' or 'Because I'm the dad, that's why'?" Liz's question brought smiles all around because those who were not yet parents had at least heard this themselves when they were children. The line was well known.

"That's using your position to influence others. The parent, the manager, the teacher, the CEO—they all come with a degree of power just because of the title. However, at some point, performance had better match the title or, once again, the credibility is undermined," Liz knew she had hit home with this one. There were many managers at *REV*:Elation who wore their titles like a beauty pageant sash.

"The other thing to remember about these first three is the response they yield from the followers. When faced with these types of influence, most people will simply go along, but their hearts aren't in it. They obey, but they don't buy it," Liz continued. "Now on the other hand, the next three, when used correctly, tend to bring about commitment, or at least a greater level of genuine following."

"I can totally see that about **personality**," mentioned Josh. "There's a woman in our department, Catherine, who just seems to attract people. She has this magnetic personality, chipper and friendly and genuine, that makes people flock to her. She never has to ask twice for help when she needs it. I've always been amazed at how effective she is."

"Well, around here those personality traits are rare," teased Dee. "And I'm not surprised that she has a department full of guys eating out of her hand."

"The next one is tied to it," Liz jumped in before Josh could respond to Dee's jab. "Think of **liaison** influence as 'guilt by association,' but in a positive way. People tend to give power to the associates of powerful people, sometimes without even thinking of it. There are dangers in using this, as Dirk and Rani have demonstrated, but it can be used effectively as well."

"And I supposed the **expert** influence is just as the name implies … after all, don't they always say that knowledge is power?" offered Isabella.

"Exactly right! But remember that these sources of power all tie back to the game being played and have some relationship to the original three 'game balls' of resources, information, and people. Also, it is important to note that each of these power sources has an appropriate time and a place. None of them is bad unless they overused or used inappropriately," Liz said, then began wrapping up the discussion. "It sounds like you all have absorbed a lot in this meeting. Would anyone like to carry on the conversation in a more favorable setting? I saw a coffeehouse with live jazz a couple of blocks down. Anyone interested?"

Everyone nodded their agreement. It was later than they had realized, but they had been enjoying the conversation. They had also enjoyed seeing the applications and assistance their new project manager was bringing to the table.

Anne was the last one to leave the room. She paused for a moment to speak to Liz before she left the meeting room.

"Liz, thanks for helping us … for helping me. We've all had it pretty rough on this product launch for months. We respected Vic for lasting as long as he did. You've reminded me that I still have a lot to learn about office politics and about myself. I'll try to be a bit more open-minded. You really do seem to have our best interests at heart."

"Thanks, Anne," responded Liz. "I'll try my hardest not to let any of you down."

Chapter 7

Liz began noticing a marked difference in her team over the next several days. They were all more observant to what was going on around them. They were paying attention to apparent political games and were able to identify why some of the games were occurring, as well as what was motivating them. Others in the organization were also starting to take notice of Liz's project team, namely because the previously embattled team was now calling them on the carpet for playing politics.

Liz was pleased that she was making headway with each of the five individuals on her team, and she was relieved that she was able to add the kind of value that Frank had wanted her to bring to the table. That is, until the phone call arrived.

"Ms. Meredith, would you please come to Mr. Truman's office?" Liz recognized the voice of Frank's administrative assistant, Bonnie. "He would like to speak with you immediately."

Liz headed up to Frank's office, uncertain what created the need for an impromptu meeting. Bonnie ushered her into his office and closed the door.

"What's up, Frank?" Liz started the conversation. When

Frank looked up from his desk, he looked weary and beat up.

"Liz, please tell me why I shouldn't end our little arrangement today and send you back to your investigation business?" Frank's directness shocked Liz, who was left speechless for a few moments. After staring at Frank in disbelief, Liz finally regained her composure.

"Frank, can you back up a little bit and tell me why you even asked me that question?" Liz did not like being accused of failing at anything, so Frank's question was both unexpected and unappreciated.

"Sure, Liz. I just had to listen to Dirk Runnells for two straight hours, telling me how you are undermining the success of your own project, and how you are poisoning the minds of your entire project team against this organization. Do you agree with his assessment?"

"Undermining success? Poisoning minds? Frank, you have me at a disadvantage here. Where are these accusations coming from? My team and I barely see Dirk Runnells, let alone deal directly with him. He's always conveniently unavailable when we do need him. Why is he coming to you?" Liz felt the color rise in her cheeks, belying her normally fair complexion.

"Tell me this, Liz. Did you tell your team that playing politics was morally justifiable? Did you specifically undermine the credibility of Rani Blackburg, a consultant whom Dirk Runnells values very highly? Did you really refer to the people who play politics in this company as SOBs?" Frank kept an even voice, but Liz could tell he was pretty agitated.

"Yes, Frank, but you need to understand the context ..." Liz began.

"Screw the context, Liz! I brought you here to improve the state of relationships here at *REV*:Elation, not to make them even worse! Dirk wants me to fire you. And if you say his accusations are correct, then I need to know why we should even continue with this conversation."

"Now look here, Frank," Liz began, leaning over his desk

and looking him directly in the eye. "For starters, you *begged* me to come here and help teach your employees effective office politics management. I've made great strides with five people who were either too cynical to care or too scared to defend their own project, let alone their own actions."

"Yes, but …" Frank attempted to reignite his indictment.

"I'm *not* done yet." It was Liz's turn to interrupt, and by her tone, Frank knew better than to try to speak until she was done. He had seen this look a couple of times during their college years, and he knew better than to say anything until Liz had completed her thoughts.

"Second, I've been here for only a couple of months. You expected me to wave some magic wand and have all of your problems solved instantly? How naïve can one executive be? Handling office politics is a process, Frank, and I am mentoring my team—*your* team—through the steps of dealing with political issues. Unlike your normal corporate culture, which rushes everything through without consideration for timing or readiness, I make sure one step in the process is sufficiently understood and mastered before I move on to the next one. I thought that's why you selected me to handle your problems.

"Third, I'm not your enemy here. From what I can tell, Dirk Runnells is. He and his evil minions have been attempting to derail this product launch for months. It's no wonder he's upset with me, because my team and I are suddenly turning the tables on some of his efforts and beginning to make some progress toward a successful end result."

Liz was clearly not amused, and Frank was left looking fairly dumbfounded. As CEO, he was unaccustomed to people talking back to him, outside of Vic. There was another long, uncomfortable silence as the two scrutinized each other across the desk. Frank broke the quiet barrier.

"About Dirk—can you prove it?" Clearly, Frank had heard rumblings of this accusation before, but he would need to see hard, clear evidence before confronting another executive on something this serious.

"As a matter of fact, I'm confident that I can. Most of what I've uncovered so far would fall into the category of hear-say or circumstantial evidence. But Dirk, while a shrewd politician, is actually pretty sloppy when it comes to 'disposing of bodies.' I am fairly sure I can prove to you that he wants to see this project fail and figure out why. How long and how much space are you willing to give me?"

"I'll tell Dirk that you're on probation. He'll probably buy it for now. That will give you a few weeks, at least until the executive presentation for the product launch. Liz, be careful on this. You know how protective some executives can be of their careers and their domains."

"Don't worry, Frank, I've dealt with people worse than Dirk Runnells. I'll get things figured out, and I'll continue to keep my team moving forward."

"Don't let me down, Liz. It's getting ugly with him." Frank had a look of seriousness that concerned Liz, but also challenged her.

On her way back to her office, Liz reflected on how this situation had exploded on her. Had she let her guard down? Was one of her team actually turning against her? After all, the information that Frank had shared with her could only have come from one of their project team meetings. Dee was still defensive and outspoken. Could she have tipped her hand to Dirk? What about Anne? Was her quiet aversion to politics just an act? Or could it be Josh? He was the only one of the team with a direct tie to Dirk through his dealings with Rani. Being a good corporate investigator had bred in Liz a healthy sense of paranoia; however, in this case Liz concluded the information that Frank had shared was probably the by-product of simple communication channels.

She shrugged it off. Now was not the time for unbridled neuroses. She had seen too many managers go down in flames after a meeting like the one she had with Frank. They became so obsessed with flushing out the perceived traitors from within their ranks that they took their eye off the ball and forgot the bigger picture of why they were there. After all, her team had been open and receptive to her coaching. She didn't think any of them would deliberately try to undermine her efforts to be successful on the project. She was a very good judge of character, and she knew that remaining objective about the situation would be important as the project continued forward.

Liz was still thinking about what had happened with Frank when the next team meeting occurred a few days later. The only conclusion she had reached was that her team was a little too open about their communications stemming from their project meetings. Their comfort with their newfound knowledge had motivated some confidence to degrees Liz had not expected. She was pleased that they were progressing, but she knew that now was the time to cover the next element of GUST.

As the team congregated in the East Conference Room, Liz could tell there was a higher level of energy. Her team had been communicating with her on a regular basis, and simply being able to identify political games and understand them was empowering. Even Anne was developing a greater level of courage in dealing with project issues, although her oppressive manager was still a thorn in her side.

The team provided their project updates in a timely fashion. The product launch had reached a critical point where the delays already incurred were beginning to have an adverse impact on the overall project and were becoming visible to the rest of the organization. However, many of the team members were finally making headway, which came as a great relief to Liz.

Without much fanfare, Liz transitioned into the weekly mentoring session on dealing with office politics. The team quickly reviewed the points covered to date, sharing some examples and discussing some new issues that had arisen. Liz then turned to the flip chart and added the next piece to the puzzle.

> **Office Politics 101**
> *Game*
> *Understand*
> *Strategy*
> *T*

"**Strategy**?" questioned Dee, now with more eagerness in her voice than sarcasm. "This ought to be good."

"It is," assured Liz. "Strategy is where you start to plan what you are going to do about the political game in which you are embroiled. But, like anything else, there's a process to be followed, or you can find yourself pushing your way through blindly."

"A process?" pondered Shay. "Why do I sense another acronym coming on?"

"You know me too well, Shay," Liz admitted as she turned another page in the flip chart.

> **Political Strategy: RACE**
> *Roles*
> *Approach*
> *Character*
> *Evidence*

"Why do we need yet another process?" moaned Dee.

"No kidding," echoed Anne. "If I'm going to have to play politics, let's just get it over with."

"You've spent all this time learning how to understand the political game. So wouldn't it make sense to use that understanding to figure out what you need to do before you try to do it?" Liz once again took the opportunity to turn her team's questions into a learning experience for them. "For example, if the person who is initiating the political game is a snake, you may need to proceed with caution in whatever strategy you take. That's where the **Roles** come in."

"That makes some sense," admitted Dee, a little embarrassed that she had jumped on Liz so quickly over this issue. "I suppose it would help us to think about whether our political adversary is a snake, an ostrich, or a bear. Then we can tailor our approach accordingly. For the longest time, I've been perceiving Mark Washington as a snake. Now I'm realizing that he's actually more of a bear politician. He just wants to keep his department intact, so he's willing to do whatever he needs to ensure that happens. It's really not about his ego at all."

Liz acknowledged Dee's recognition of Mark's role, then she led the team through a quick brainstorming session on suggestions for handling each of the three kinds of politicians. When they were finished, the result looked like this:

Snake	Ostrich	Bear
Cover your tail … always *Share only necessary information; don't provide too much ammo they can use against you later* *Consider the snake's allies and channels of communication; watch how you talk around their friends*	*Stress the importance of engaging and the impacts to the team* *Address fears and help overcome them* *Provide a safe environment to express and vent* *Don't force into a corner; keep them at ease*	*Act logically and ethically* *Balance facts and data with relationships & communication* *Show the bear you have their team's interest at heart, too* *Point to the big picture*

"I don't know about the rest of you, but I've been having pretty good luck with just calling people on the carpet when I see them playing politics," Josh continued the conversation. Isabella agreed, noting that people seemed to drop their game-playing when they were accused of engaging in office politics.

"You may be winning the battle, only to lose the war later," cautioned Liz to her team's surprise. "That's why your **Approach** is so critical. Knowing how to identify a political game when it is happening is a great skill to have. Even better, you are now able to analyze and understand the players and underlying motives. However, simply calling somebody on the carpet for playing politics when you see it happening may not always be the best approach."

"Why not?" asked Anne and Isabella, at the same time.

Anne carried the line of questioning further. "Isn't our goal to end the political game, Liz? If we can do that simply by pointing it out when it's occurring, why wouldn't that be good enough?"

"Those are very good questions, Anne." Liz tried especially hard to sound encouraging, given the difficult time she had getting Anne to acknowledge that playing politics had its benefits. "However, people don't always behave the way we think they do. As ethical, logical people, we sometimes assume that everybody operates on the same playing field, but it just isn't so. Simply calling them on the carpet for playing politics may force them to make their political games more covert. As with every other aspect of politics, any given strategy rarely constitutes a blanket approach."

"Great, how many people have we angered?" wondered Shay aloud, echoing the thoughts of everybody else in the room.

"I'm sure you've angered a few," Liz acknowledged honestly. "But you've also put quite a few people on notice that you are aware of their political games and are not going to put up with them any more. That's not necessarily a bad thing. However, you really need to consider whether your approach should be a direct attack or whether it should be more covert and indirect.

Only you will know the answer to that question. However, choose the incorrect approach, and you could create even more problems later. The best way to decide what to do is to consider if your approach aligns with your political adversaries' approach. You want to address their behaviors *and* your desired results effectively."

"That makes sense," Josh interjected. "When I openly accused Rani Blackburg of playing politics to keep our documentation from being approved, she changed her tune in the meeting very quickly, so I took advantage of the moment to get the documentation's approval pushed through. The look on her face meant that I was going to be in trouble later, though."

"That's a good example of overt political maneuvers, Josh," Liz observed. "Sometimes there's safety in numbers, and leveraging that fact occasionally makes it acceptable to indict politicians publicly for their game-playing."

"And other times?" Dee asked.

"As you have guessed, there are times when it pays to be covert. If the situation could backfire on you, or if the 'other side' has a stronger ripple of influence than you do, you may have to rely on more 'behind the scenes' activities," Liz responded. "It's like on reality television shows, when people build alliances or make deals. Whichever route you choose, the trick is to stay off the political radar screen for as long as possible and still accomplish your goal."

"That makes sense," Anne affirmed. Then, glancing at the flip chart, she continued. "This may sound like a funny question coming from me, but how does character fit into playing politics?"

"**Character** actually applies on two levels," Liz explained. "First, you should consider the character of your political opponent. If he or she has a reputation for acting consistently and playing aboveboard, and the political game being played does not appear to align with that normally high integrity, it may open up the opportunity to hold a simple conversation. There may be other forces at play—things you are totally unaware of—that are affecting the situation and the behavior. If the person is not known for integrity, then you may need to proceed with caution."

"And the second part of character?" Isabella interjected.

"Just make sure you don't sink to the level of your political adversary," Liz responded simply. "Politics is a dangerous game to play, even if your motives are purely benevolent. Once you have a reputation for acting politically, regardless of the circumstances and the rationale, people will look at you in a different light. Sometimes favorably, sometimes not."

"**Evidence** sounds a little heavy-handed," commented Dee, moving on to the last item on the list.

"Actually, this is the biggest strategy which is often overlooked yet is so critical to political success," Liz said. "Often, we let emotion drive our political resolutions. The key to evidence is taking emotion out of the equation and being able to prove your point through facts and data, and the best way to prove your point is through documentation."

"As in writing things down?" Anne stated incredulously. "I'm sorry, Liz, but what is that going to do for any of us? That hardly seems very earth-shattering."

"Anne, how many of the carrots that Eve Uhlwich has dangled in front of you have been written down?" Anne's avoided eye contact was all the answer Liz needed.

"And Shay, how many of your hallway and phone conversations with Laurie are documented? You're constantly on her case to fulfill her promises, but you're always at a loss to make her deliver on them," Liz continued.

"What am I supposed to do?" Shay asked. "Should I just say, 'Wait a second, Laurie, which of us is writing this conversation down?' It hardly seems feasible to take minutes for every conversation I have." His retort was greeted with nods around the room. Clearly, the team was struggling with the importance of documentation.

"No, you don't have to take visible notes for every hallway

conversation," assured Liz. "When I have a conversation with another person, including each of you, I almost always follow it up with a summary email. At the end of the email, I will ask the recipient if I captured the conversation—mostly decisions and action items—correctly, with the caveat that if they do not respond with a correction or clarification within a timely manner, that I will proceed with the assumption that I captured our conversation accurately. It puts the responsibility on the other person to clarify if anything is incorrect."

"I could certainly see where that approach would be helpful," Dee came to Liz's rescue. "I've been using something similar with Mark Washington, and it's actually been helpful at building our business relationship. He's still very possessive about business information that may threaten his department or position, but I've found that simply acknowledging his point of view through an email gets me light years ahead of where I used to be with him."

Isabella added that she had been saving all of her emails with Michael Vanderpol because he continued to be difficult on providing resources for the marketing plan.

The team agreed to hold off on further open accusations of political behavior and take more time to assess each situation before deciding what to do next. Each team member also vowed to begin documenting everything related to their project and their careers. Applying the strategy of GUST would soon prove to be beneficial for Liz and the whole team.

Chapter 8

Liz was still bothered by her discussion with Frank. To have chastised her for doing the job for which he hired her was one thing, but to have done so after rarely checking in since she had arrived was frustrating.

She decided not to let it get to her; after all, her interaction with Frank was also a political game. The ultimate opponent was obvious: Dirk Runnells wielded a lot of power—too much in Liz's estimation—and he shared some of it with his designated corporate groupies who carried out his bidding.

The game in this situation was pretty straightforward. Dirk was manipulating information by using Liz's own words against her. Additionally, he was manipulating people through his relationship with Frank, as well as through the managers her team was having conflicts with.

Liz knew her job was easier when she was on the outside looking in on office politics. As a corporate investigator, she never let herself get this emotionally involved with any employee or activity. She came in, did her job, found the dirt, turned it over, and got out. Quick, clean, straightforward. Sometimes it took a couple of weeks. Sometimes it took a couple of years. But she was always successful, primarily because she was always on the outside looking in. This assignment was different. Her team really counted on her. They needed her to be able to deliver. They had been burned too many times by office politics, and it had bred different reactions in each of them over time. From Anne's repression to Dee's aggression, many of the employees at **REV**:Elation had developed unhealthy approaches to the toxic relationships that had developed. And in the midst of it all, Liz was making progress. In some ways, however, Liz's own vulnerabilities were coming into play. One of the things she disliked about being an investigator was not being able to integrate herself with the company or its employees. Perhaps this project was letting Liz know that some degree of emotional involvement with her work was acceptable after all.

Liz pulled herself back into the objective analysis of her situation. She had identified the game, and it definitely involved manipulating resources, information, and people. Understanding all of the details of the game seemed less straightforward. Liz was obviously threatening Dirk Runnells' turf. Was he up to something more than simply building a corporate dynasty? Why was he avoiding her? Was he fearful of her or just working against her behind her back? Who else was working with him to undermine Liz's credibility? She had her suspicions.

She knew that Dirk did not respect Frank, and that he was bypassing Frank completely in an attempt to build relationships with the board of directors. That had to be the issue. Dirk wanted to become CEO, and the only way to do so was to make the company's largest product launch fail in such a way that it would look like Frank's fault. After all, Frank had hired Vic, who was unable to complete the task, and he also had hired Liz. If both of Frank's choices for project manager failed, it would be fairly easy to blame a disastrous product launch on Frank.

Then a thunderbolt hit Liz. Vic Elliott! Why hadn't she thought to contact Vic and talk to him directly? While politics had gotten the better of him, he still might have valuable insights for Liz . Obviously Frank had not told her the entire story about his Chief Operating Officer—so maybe there was more he wasn't telling her that Vic would know. It was time to do some outside research.

• • •

On another floor in another department of *REV*:Elation, Anne Ericsen was finally meeting with Eve, in a last-ditch effort to get promoted. The two had planned to meet earlier to discuss a plan for Anne's performance and career path, but Eve always backed out at the last minute, citing "important business matters." This time, Anne had stayed late in the office the night before and had checked Eve's schedule through the corporate email and scheduling software. Eve was a creature of habit, always arriving and leaving at the same time each day. Anne noticed that there were no meetings scheduled at the beginning of Eve's day, so she set up a meeting when she knew Eve would not have time either to respond to it or avoid it.

Anne also made sure she was in the office a full hour before Eve would arrive. Anne checked, and Eve's phone was not blinking, meaning that there were no voicemails that Eve could use as an excuse.

Anne previously had contacted Human Resources, where she learned of a policy that any female or minority employee who perceived inequity in his or her advancement could formally request a written performance advancement plan of their supervisor, with the objective-based, quantitative results tracked by Human Resources themselves. Anne studied all facets of the policy, and even leveraged a service representative within HR to help her prepare for the meeting.

As Eve arrived, Anne followed her directly into her office.

"I'm sorry, Anne. I'm just too busy to meet with you. I have an important meeting with the department managers first thing this morning. I'm already late," Eve attempted to look harried enough to be believable.

"Eve, your schedule indicated that you were free, and I know that those meetings are organized through the email system. Could you have been mistaken on the day? I actually scheduled this meeting time with you because I saw you were available," Anne used the same air of innocence that Eve generally leveraged on her.

Eve grumbled something about a simple misunderstanding and sat down. "OK, it seems you have something that you view important enough to discuss with me right now. Let's get this over with."

"Well, Eve, I think we can take our time. I scheduled the entire hour," Anne responded evenly and coolly. Then she proceeded to lay out the entire performance evaluation plan in writing: the rationale and the process, as well as the fact that her plan and this meeting were both sanctioned by Human Resources. Eve attempted various maneuvers to wiggle out of providing quantitative objectives for Anne's promotion, but Anne corralled her boss into compliance by keeping the conversation on track and hinting at how much of a waste of time it would be to involve Human Resources in a matter that Anne was confident that "two mature professionals" could handle on their own. In the end, Eve signed on the dotted line. Anne ensured that the forms made it to Human Resources by personally walking them over to the service representative with whom she had worked earlier. She would have a lot to report later that day at the team meeting.

• • •

The team meetings were becoming more energized. With the project implementation date looming, Liz was now requiring meetings with her core team up to three times each week. In addition, the team was always anxious to discuss the skills they had applied in effectively handling politics. The one lesson they had learned quickly was that "one size fits all" is a myth when dealing with office politics. A technique used successfully in one situation may lead to disastrous results in a different one. It was this exact issue they were discussing when Liz walked in the room.

"It would appear as though you've already stumbled upon the 'T' in our GUST metaphor," she said, smiling as she produced the now-familiar flip chart:

Office Politics 101

Game

Understand

Strategy

Take Action

"Yes, but actually putting things into practice is a lot harder than simply analyzing and strategizing about them," admitted Josh.

Isabella nodded in agreement. "It seems that when the rubber hits the road, I have a few successes, but more often than not, I fall flat on my face and make matters worse."

"Can any of you give me an example of that happening?" Liz asked her team with genuine concern.

"I can," responded Shay. "As many of you know, Laurie Traiger is constantly expecting us to follow corporate protocol in all situations, whether or not it makes sense. Because we've been preparing for the product testing phase of this project, I've been setting up the testing lab room, where the people who will be using our new product will try to break it before it is released."

"Don't tell me that she's not going to let us have the space for the lab?" interrupted Dee fiercely to Shay's sheepish yet sullen nod. "She truly is the business progress preventer. We can't release the product if we don't test it in the lab!"

"Calm down, Dee," chided Isabella. "Shay, what happened?"

"Well, first she claimed she didn't have the space. When I produced floor plans from the Facilities department, showing her exactly which areas were vacated and for how long, she became very cold and said we would need to discuss it later. The next thing I know, I'm being called into my manager's office and yelled at for repeatedly ignoring company policies and chains of command," Shay punctuated his story with a strong and indignant huff.

"Well, you know Laurie," Josh interjected. "She will use passive aggression and non-compliance to lull you into a sense of complacency. Then she attacks when your back is turned. And she hates being challenged with facts that make her look wrong or bad." The team agreed on that point. It seemed all of them at one time or another had dealt with this approach from Laurie Traiger.

"OK, so you're dealing with a bit of a sociopath here, right Shay?" Liz began. "But knowing what you know about her, why did you think she would respond any differently given that you knew your approach would blindside her and put her on the defensive?"

"I guess I just wanted to resolve the issue so badly, I was willing to try anything to get that floor space," Shay admitted.

"Why don't we try a different approach to taking action?" Liz suggested. "You realize that you need to STOP before you can go, don't you?"

Seeing their confused looks, Liz moved to the flip chart, turned to a clean sheet of paper and wrote the following:

Taking Action - STOP to go
Support
Timing
Outcome
Passion

"Before you can take action on a political battle, you need to assess your battlefield, as well as your own arsenal," Liz continued. "Looking at **Support**, it's always good to think about your stakeholders before you go into battle. Consider the people you analyzed during the 'Understand' phase of GUST. Who are the players? Who supports you? Who is against you? Who may be apathetic or otherwise neutral about what you are trying to accomplish? Who are you just not sure about? Are they overt or covert in their response to you? The key question you have to ask is whether you have enough support to meet your goal. If you don't, can you muster enough support to do what you want to get done? Case in point, Shay: Did you consider talking to your department manager about the space issue with Laurie before you approached Facilities to obtain the information?"

"But that could mean thinking about dozens of people, Liz," Dee moaned. "Sometimes decisions need to be made on the fly, and you don't have time to do this analysis."

"I'm glad you brought that up, Dee, because the next item to consider before taking action is **Timing**. How quickly do you need to act? How much time do you have to give due diligence to your decisions and actions? Is it a good time emotionally for all of the players to try to move forward?" Liz continued the line of thinking. "If the timing isn't right, you may want to consider holding off on action, if that is an option. In the case of your earlier example, if the number of stakeholders is too large, and the decision needs to be made immediately, it might be a red flag to slow things down a little."

"But what about **Outcomes**?" Anne asked. "Shouldn't we already know what we want by that time?"

"Yes," responded Liz. "You know what you want the final result to be. Generally speaking, you want to win the political conflict, or at least resolve it. But what does that resolution look like? Are you willing to sacrifice the relationship with the person in order to get your way? Are you endangering relationships with others if you win the political game? What outcomes beyond your political conflict are you seeking? If you are uncertain of this, you may need to rethink *why* you are engaged in this political battle. Josh, your recent encounters with Rani are a good example of this. The outcome of obtaining the signatures comes with a side effect—Rani's increased hostility."

"The **Passion** aspect intrigues me," added Shay. "I didn't know we were allowed to be passionate about anything here at **REV**:Elation."

"Not allowed?" Liz was incredulous. "Shay—and this goes for the rest of you, too—if you're not passionate about what you are fighting for, then you probably should just pack it up now and not bother. Passion is what fuels the desire to make it work. It's what gives you the courage to engage in the conflict. What gets you excited at work? I would hope it's the project we've been working on together." Liz found that she was giving that soapbox speech as much to herself as she was to her team.

The intensity of her answer caught her team off guard, but they knew she was correct in her assessment. They all had a vested interest in seeing this project succeed, and all of them now took the setbacks personally.

After the meeting adjourned, each team member went back to finish up some work before going home.

As Josh Matthews arrived at his desk, Dirk Runnells was there waiting for him.

"What can I do for you, Dirk?" Josh offered in as friendly of a voice as he could muster, given the contempt he felt for the Chief Operating Officer.

"You're coming with me to my office … NOW!" Dirk hissed in a threatening voice. "I have some issues to discuss with you."

Chapter 9

"Is this really necessary?" Shay Pradhan asked his department manager, Anita.

"Shay, when Laurie Traiger calls with a threat to have you fired and my department written up for not following company policy, then it's time for a meeting," Anita was curt in her response. Then she softened. "Look, I know you were trying to do what's best for your project, Shay, and I generally applaud your out-of-the-box approach solutions; however, company policies exist for a reason. Laurie's accusations are serious. Now let's go."

"OK, let me grab my folder first," Shay said, pulling the binder containing all of the documentation he'd been keeping on his communication with Laurie.

When Shay and Anita arrived in the conference room, they found a compliance officer from the company's Legal department, as well as a Human Resources representative; Laurie, however, was not yet in the room. Shay was beginning to realize how serious Laurie's charges were.

The four individuals engaged in small talk while they waited for Laurie to arrive. Shay was relieved when Liz walked into the conference room. "Don't mind me," she told the others. "I'm merely here as an interested bystander." She gave Shay a wink and a reassuring smile when nobody else was looking.

Five minutes after the meeting was scheduled to begin, Laurie came rushing into the conference room, looking harried and disorganized as usual.

"Thank you all for coming," Laurie began very officiously. "It's always unfortunate when we have to meet under these circumstances; however, we cannot have renegades and loose cannons going around usurping company policies, can we?" She shot a smug look of self-righteous satisfaction at Shay.

The compliance officer and Human Resource representative nodded in agreement as Laurie launched into her version of all of Shay's violations of equipment and space procurement. When she began to exonerate her own department as mere victims of Shay's reckless flaunting of company policy, Shay could keep quiet no longer.

"Um, Laurie, may I add some information here?" he began quietly.

"I don't see what you could possibly have that would be relevant, but if you must speak, now is as good of a time as any," Laurie said, her nasally voice taking on an accusatory tone that made him cringe internally. He pulled out two packets of paper and handed them to the participants in the room, thinking how glad he was now that he had made extra copies.

"I've reviewed the company policies, as well as the specific department policies that Laurie has accused me of breaking," Shay started. "It is true that I made procurements for my project team and expensed them back to the company through my timesheet, bypassing Laurie's Help Desk department in order to get the equipment I needed."

"Admitting the problem is the first step to solving it," Laurie interrupted condescendingly. Shay ignored her as he continued.

"Both Corporate and Help Desk policies provide several alternatives, however, as noted in the first packet of papers I've just handed you. If you will note in Section III, Item B,

Subarticles 3 through 5 of the Employee Handbook, it states that '*an employee who has made every attempt through channels to procure an item unsuccessfully may in turn purchase the item on his own with the consent of either a functional manager or a project manager, depending on the ownership of the equipment and the need in question.*'"

"Are you accusing my department of not doing its job, Shay?" Laurie did not like the turn that Shay had made, and she began speaking even more quickly. "This meeting is no place for smoke and mirrors. My department is working very hard and makes every effort to provide service of the highest quality and timing." Shay ignored her and continued.

"You will notice in the second packet that I've provided a list of emails between Laurie and myself, including summaries of phone conversations to Laurie which I emailed to her, which all indicate that I *have* made the efforts required in this policy before I made the decision to pursue the procurement by myself," Shay kept his voice steady and calm. Laurie, on the other hand, began rambling about "inconsequential detail" and "cheap theatrics" and "getting everybody off task" until the compliance officer politely asked her to be quiet while he read Shay's documentation.

As they finished reading, the tone in the room began to shift. Shay handed out his third and fourth stapled packets of information. He directed the members in the room to read the first packet of new information, which included all of Liz's written approvals for purchases, the receipts, and the expense system documentation, all perfectly in order.

"The final piece of documentation," Shay summarized, "is from Laurie's own department. I worked with one of her Help Desk advisors over a weekend to document how the work flows in their department and to implement a tracking system. Laurie is correct that her department does have a very good procurement success rate, except for the purchase orders that she handles herself." Shay had worked with the individual in the department to chart each advisor's turnaround time, his or her success rate at solving the problem the first time, and the satisfaction ratings received. The department as a whole was averaging over 90 percent success on all orders. After showing them the department's performance, he indicated the final page, which had isolated Laurie's performance on these same measures. The results were dismal. Lost purchase orders, rework, and complaints were rampant. With Laurie's results removed, the team's results were over 98 percent successful.

"You certainly cannot believe this is accurate," Laurie began animatedly to the attendees from Legal and Human Resources. "Shay had to have made up these numbers to cover his own tail." She turned to Shay and sneered, "Breaking the rules is one thing, but lying is definitely going to get you fired."

There was an uncomfortable silence in the room that lasted about a minute. The Compliance Officer and Human Resources representative exchanged glances.

"Shay, Anita, Liz, you may leave," the representative from Human Resources stated quietly. "We are sorry to have wasted your time. Shay, thank you for sharing your side of the story on this issue. I think we can consider this problem resolved … at least where you're concerned." She gave a hard glance toward Laurie. "For other people, issues are only just beginning."

Shay, Anita, and Liz quickly filtered out of the room as Laurie began ranting about fairness and spin doctoring and manipulating data. The compliance officer escorted them out.

"Sorry you had to go through all that, Shay," he conceded. "Your research and documentation were very thorough, and I appreciate how well you kept your cool in there. It was easy to see which side was more credible."

The compliance officer returned to the room as Anita congratulated Shay and excused herself to another meeting. When both were out of sight, Shay and Liz gave each other a quick high five before walking quickly up the hall.

• • •

"I'm sorry, Michael, but we were actually able to create the marketing plan ourselves, without the input from the Marketing department, but thank you for calling to check up on us," Isabella Gonzalez said. She had been waiting for this phone call from Michael Vanderpol for weeks, ever since Michael had stonewalled the use of two of his people to help with the marketing plan on the product launch.

"You can't create a marketing plan without input from my department," Michael stated matter-of-factly. "Why were we not included?"

"Michael, if you recall, we tried to include you months ago. We had all of the approvals in place to use your staff. For whatever reason, you neglected our request for resources," Isabella reminded him firmly yet politely.

"I demand that you redo the plan, then." Michael was obviously not happy about being bypassed or overlooked in his area of expertise.

"Redo the plan? From scratch? Are you kidding?" Isabella's voice sounded incredulous. "Do you realize how much work has gone into this already? The number of hours spent on it? You can't be serious, Michael."

"Totally serious," Michael deadpanned over the phone. "You will begin meeting with representatives from my Market Segmentation and my Promotions teams on Monday, and you will continue meeting with them until there is a marketing plan that they approve. Got it?"

"I guess, but Liz will not be happy that you are delaying her product launch. After all, we tried to get resources from you earlier," Isabella said, resigning herself to the inevitable.

"She'll just have to deal with that, as will you," Michael snarled. "Obviously, I'm going to have to provide you with resources from here on out to keep you from running wild. I'll expect a status report from the team in two weeks."

Click.

Isabella smiled. She didn't think it was necessary to tell

Michael that the marketing piece had been delayed in the project plan for another month due to anticipated launch issues. She also didn't think it necessary to inform him that the "draft press release" regarding the marketing plan's impending announcement was much more draft than it was release. Was it her fault that he assumed that it was a real press release that was about to be announced? The bottom line was that she finally had her Marketing resources, and that they would now easily be able to finalize the real marketing plan and meet the deadline with no difficulty.

. . .

"Rani, may I speak to you?" Josh caught up to Rani Blackburg as she was heading toward the elevator.

"I'm not sure we have anything to discuss, Mr. Matthews," Rani said, her voice icily formal. "You made it perfectly clear in the last meeting that my 'political behaviors' were unacceptable in your upstanding little world. I wouldn't want you to soil your reputation by being seen with me."

"Yes, Rani, about that exchange at the meeting a couple of weeks ago, that's sort of what I wanted to talk to you about," Josh began.

"Look, you got your signatures, Josh. You don't need to rub it in. Just don't expect any favors from me in the future." She gestured for Josh to either get in the elevator or get out of the path of the door so it could close.

"It doesn't need to be like this," Josh said as he stepped into the elevator with her. "I wanted to apologize to you for making those comments publicly. It was unprofessional and uncalled for."

"Oh, so now you don't think I'm a 'political little snake-in-the-grass'? I believe that's the term you used, wasn't it?"

"Well, no Rani, I still think you are political, and I still think that your actions are questionable. I'm apologizing for making the comments publicly."

"That's not an acceptable apology in my book," stated Rani

coldly as the elevator doors opened and she walked off. "Good day."

"So, you're willing to let a business relationship go down the tubes simply because you didn't get your way on one project decision? Doesn't that seem a little juvenile?" Josh appeared to have hit an unwanted bull's-eye with his choice of words. Rani spun around quickly, her eyes blazing.

"For the record, Josh: This project is going to fail anyway. Technical documentation or not, there is no way that Dirk Runnells will let this ill-conceived product launch. And that so-called project manager of yours will be thrown out of here like yesterday's garbage!" Rani was becoming quite animated.

"Whoa, whoa, whoa," Josh responded calmly. "Where did you get that load of information? Certainly none of that has been communicated to our project team. I know that you and Dirk have expressed your concerns to me about the product's feasibility, but your prognosis sounds a little fatalistic."

Rani suddenly looked alarmed. "I've already said too much," she blurted as she rushed off, leaving Josh standing awkwardly alone, wondering what had gone wrong with his attempted apology. He figured he could have handled it better, but he still wondered about the giant mood shift at the end.

• • •

"Hi, Mark, do you have a minute?" Dee Connors popped her head into Mark Washington's office.

"Yes, hi there, I was hoping you'd stop by." Mark looked up from his desk.

"Mark, I have some questions about this impact report our team is working on for our product launch, and I could really use your input. As you know, the launch is occurring in a few weeks, but in reviewing our project impacts, I noticed some things that could have an adverse impact on your department. These are issues we did not consider during design, but now I think they will have a bearing on you and your team."

"Really?" Mark looked concerned. "May I see what they are?"

Dee carefully reviewed each of the impacts with Mark, ensuring that he not only understood the issue at hand, but also why Dee thought it would affect his department. She had been very careful to keep the information on an objective level, to show specific facts and data, and to keep emotion out of the conversation. After all, no manager likes to find out at the last minute that his department will be impacted by another project.

"In conclusion, Mark, I have some ideas on how to mitigate these issues, and I've brought along some recommendations, but I'd really appreciate some feedback from you as opposed to just 'throwing it over the wall' like we usually do here at *REV*:Elation. Is now a good time, or do we need to schedule another meeting?" Dee smiled inwardly as she thought of how badly their earlier exchanges went.

"Actually, now is as good of a time as any," Mark responded. "I appreciate your sharing these impacts with me, Dee. If we had been surprised by these at launch time, it would have shut down our department and thrown us into chaos. It seems to me that I have some notes from our executive retreat a few months ago that could shed some light on impacts 23, 45, and 47 from your list. Ah yes, here it is."

Mark pulled the binder from his drawer and laid it out on his desk where both he and Dee could look at it. As Dee had suspected months ago, it contained information that could have negated the need for this meeting now, but she and Mark were not exactly on pleasant speaking terms back then. The important thing was that he was sharing it with her now.

"Yes, I think this could work, Dee," confirmed Mark with a smile. "Again, I can't thank you enough for taking the time to walk through this with me. My team will be more prepared to handle the changes coming through when your project implements."

"My pleasure, Mark," responded Dee. "In the future, I'll keep the lines of communication open between our two departments.

It sounds like we could have some more of these overlaps occurring on future projects. I appreciate your time."

As Dee walked away from Mark's office, she reflected on how his game—withholding information—had changed once she had taken the time to realize his motivations for maintaining control over his department and formulated an appropriate strategy for his bearish approach. She knew that he responded well to deadlines, so she best would be able to reach resolution if she waited until closer to the implementation date, but not too close that potential problems could not be fixed. Finally being able to see the notes from the Executive Retreat gave her the opportunity to put together some of the big picture items that had been missing from her project until now.

I can't wait to tell Liz, she thought to herself. *We finally were able to get a win over Mark Washington.* Then she mentally corrected herself. *Actually, we were able to share a win* with *Mark Washington.*

• • •

"Anne … my office … *NOW!*" Eve looked visibly agitated and was unable to construct a full sentence.

"I'll be right there," Anne sighed. She knew that the promotion list had already been distributed to the managers and would be made public to the company in a few hours. While she had already proven to Human Resources that she had met all of criteria for promotion many times over, she expected that it was still premature to expect any kind of reward for performance, given how recently she had been able to get Eve to objectively document the criteria for promotion.

"Sit down," Eve ordered Anne, who complied without question as Eve slammed a stapled document down on her desk directly in front of Anne. "Do you want to explain the meaning of this?"

"It appears to be the promotion list," observed Anne, not wanting to get her hopes up but realizing something had happened to elicit this level of reaction from her supervisor.

"I know what it is," Eve exploded. "I want to know the meaning of the third notice on the second page."

Anne read the notice. And reread it. And read it a third time. She couldn't believe her eyes.

> ## Notice!
> Anne Ericsen has been promoted to
> Sr. Manager, Analysis and Design,
> filling the position left vacant earlier this year.

"Wow, Eve, I don't know what to say. I only expected a jump up one level to Supervisor or to Senior Analyst. I didn't expect them to leapfrog me up two whole levels," Anne was growing more excited while Eve was obviously seething. Then the reality of the announcement hit Anne, and a huge light bulb went on in her head.

"Hey, wait a second … Senior Manager … Why, that means I'm …"

"My boss," interrupted Eve, almost choking back tears. "Say it: you're my boss. I don't know how you pulled off this maneuver, but I'm not going to sit still for it. You don't deserve it. You haven't earned it. I won't let it happen."

With that, Eve ran out of her own office, leaving Anne alone to contemplate the impact of what had just occurred. Anne later found out that Eve took the rest of the day off. When she got back to her own desk, Anne sent an email to the project team, informing them of the announcement.

"Meet at the Coffee Bar at 5:00 today," she told them. "The first round is on me. Get there early before the shock wears off."

• • •

"You're working late." Josh Matthews almost jumped out of his skin at the sound of Dirk Runnells' voice. It was almost 10:00 at night, and he thought he was alone in the office.

"I … uh … have a few things to resolve before tomorrow's executive launch meeting," Josh stammered. "You know … to make sure things go just right, Dirk. Like we talked about earlier."

"As long as 'just right' means complete and utter failure for Liz and her team during the executive launch presentation tomorrow, then we're on the same page," Dirk whispered venomously. "I heard about your little exchange earlier with Rani. Your future success with *REV*:Elation depends on this project's failure, Josh. Don't forget it … or else."

And with that, Dirk Runnells had disappeared back into the shadows of the myriad cubicles, leaving Josh to ponder his fate.

Chapter 10

The day of the executive demonstration meeting arrived, more quickly than Liz or her team would have liked. Still, the day would not have been possible had it not been for the team's newfound knowledge about managing office politics more effectively.

Even if the project fails, thought Liz, *the team is a success. They'll be able to tackle whatever hits them from here on out.*

Still, Frank Truman had hired her not only to mentor her team on how to handle politics but also to manage the project to a successful completion. She still had to deliver on the second point, and getting the executive board's approval to proceed to the product's implementation was a critical step.

She was standing outside the executive conference suite nervously looking at her watch.

"Are you expecting somebody?" Josh Matthews asked her with a surprised tone. "I thought that only the two of us were delivering this presentation today."

"Just nervous, I guess, Josh," Liz replied in an uncharacteristically tentative voice. "I'd just like to get this over and done with. You've done a masterful job getting the product prototype ready for this demo, and if what happens in there is only half as good as what I observed yesterday, then we're a shoe-in to get the executive team's approval."

Frank's executive assistant finally opened the heavy oak doors. "They're on break, so you may go in and begin setting up," she informed them. "They will begin again in 10 minutes."

"Thank you, Bonnie," Liz responded, attempting to sound confident, but inside her stomach was churning nervously.

Liz gestured for Josh to go ahead and begin the setup. She explained she needed a few moments to psych herself up for the meeting.

"I hope Dee and Isabella deliver," she muttered under her breath when she was sure no one was within earshot.

With seconds to spare before being summoned into the conference room, Dee and Isabella arrived with another man, wearing a visitor's badge. Liz directed them to the kitchen serving area connected to the main executive conference room.

"We know what to do," Isabella assured her with the additional admonition: "Relax!"

"Inhale, exhale, repeat," Liz reminded herself as she pushed open the heavy wooden doors. As she walked into the room, she saw Frank seated at the head of the table. Something in his eyes told Liz that he was as nervous as she was. In addition to the normal set of executives, Dirk Runnells was there along with his consultant, Rani. Liz looked around the room quickly and noticed Josh still working on the prototype. He did not look happy.

"Josh, why aren't you all set up?" Liz asked under her breath. "It's showtime, and we don't get another crack at this."

"I don't know," he whispered in a panicked voice. "It's just acting weird."

"Are you ready to begin with your presentation and demonstration?" Dirk asked cordially. With a slight air of self-importance, he reminded them that their audience did not have time to spare for needless delays.

"Go along with me, Josh," Liz muttered. "I'm going to work without a net."

Before Josh could respond, Liz launched into her presentation. As had become her trademark, she walked over to the nearest flip chart, warmly thanked and welcomed her audience, and asked each executive his or her expectations of the new product her team had developed. Liz always had a knack for maintaining a commanding presence with any group, so virtually nobody noticed the three newcomers walk in the back of the room until Liz had finished her introductory comments.

"Before we begin with the formal presentation," she began. "It seemed only fitting to include a very special individual in this event, a man without whom today could never have occurred."

Dee turned on the projector that was hooked up to the additional laptop she had brought, and Isabella unveiled a working prototype of the new product, both of which had been prepared in the event of an emergency. Dirk Runnells' glare could have burned a hole through Josh, who sheepishly shrugged as if he had no idea why his role in the presentation was being commandeered.

"… and so I'd like to introduce Victor Elliott, whom many of you may remember as being the initial project manager as well as the brains behind this product," Liz said, wrapping up her introduction. "Vic will be assisting me in presenting the features of *REV*:Elation's newest product."

"I object," Dirk spoke up immediately. "This man is no longer a *REV*:Elation employee, and what we are covering today is proprietary information. Also, we only authorized the project manager to bring a single team member, not a cast of thousands."

"Loosen up, Dirk," retorted Frank impatiently. "First of all, this is not a court of law, so objecting only makes you look ridiculous. Second, Liz called me yesterday, and I confirmed with her that she could bring however many people she needed to ensure this presentation went smoothly. Third, Vic is once again a *REV*:Elation employee. I rehired him earlier this week to oversee the implementation once this product is approved and launched."

"That's a rather irresponsible move, even for a CEO, don't you think?" Dirk's voice rose in both volume and pitch as he stood up from his chair, posturing himself to tower over Frank. "This executive board has not yet even approved the solution being presented … nor do I think they will."

"Dirk, sit down and be quiet. Maybe the rest of us would like to hear what's going on. After all, you were the one preaching about how busy we 'really important people' are." When the Chairwoman of the Board publicly issues such an order that firmly, even the most difficult executive complies.

The rest of the meeting went off without a hitch. Liz and Vic masterfully traded the emcee role in a seamless presentation that left everybody in the room spellbound and convinced—well, almost everybody.

"This will never work! Can't you see that it's purely a shell game they are trying to sell you?" Dirk began to launch into a litany of reasons to discredit the team's presentation. Liz watched as the other executives began to shoot holes in his arguments. Dirk turned to Rani for support, but she was shrewd enough to recognize an intellectual slaughter and did not want to experience the carnage firsthand.

"Dirk, I think this executive board has spoken loudly and clearly on the future of this product," the Chairwoman finally stated, getting up out of her chair and putting her hand firmly on Dirk's shoulder. At this gesture, the room quieted quickly, knowing the implications of this body language. "Dirk, I'm disappointed in you. You've been presenting yourself as a proponent of moving this company forward, but based on what I've witnessed today, I think we need to meet later and discuss your future here at *REV*:Elation. Since you seem to add no value to the content of this meeting, why don't you return to your office now, and I will meet you there later."

Dirk grabbed his materials and headed for the door, his posture now a mix of deposed tyrant and scolded puppy. Rani cautiously followed him. He stopped at the door where Josh was still sitting quietly, as if to gesture him to follow as well. Josh simply got up and held the door open for him with a smile. He figured that Dirk didn't need to know that he had "tipped off" Liz about the attempted sabotage effort, and that Liz had instructed him to play along. Still, not even Liz had ever seen an executive ejected and humiliated so badly in this kind of meeting before.

Liz and her team sat quietly through the remainder of the meeting, after which they garnered the appropriate praise for their efforts. Liz encouraged Vic to take Dee, Josh, and Isabella to meet with the remainder of the team to congratulate them all on a job well done. She promised to join them later.

$$\cdot \ \cdot \ \cdot$$

In Frank's office an hour later, Liz handed in her employee badge and a stack of exit paperwork. She would inform her team at their celebration that the handoff back to Vic was intended to be a permanent one, although she guessed that many of them had already surmised as much. Frank smiled as he handed her a travel itinerary.

"How did you accomplish so much in just a few months?" he asked. He still had a look of disbelief on his face over what had transpired. "After all these years, you still surprise me."

"Good," Liz replied with a smile. "Let's keep it that way."

Frank ignored her. "Not only did you mentor a very challenging and challenged team on the finer art of handling office politics, you also successfully managed to bring the project to completion, and all the while you were recruiting my star product designer back to the company." He shook his head as if waking up from a dream. "You know, I could use somebody like you full time here at **REV**:Elation. Are you sure you have to move on? I hear Dirk's position is now open."

Liz held up the documents Frank had just handed her for her cruise and provided him with a confident yes. "But, I'm not quite through with the mentoring. I still have one person left to deal with."

"Who's left standing, Sheriff?" Frank teased with a Western drawl. "We'll gun 'em down at sunset."

"You're the only one left who still needs to be taught a lesson or two, Frank," Liz said with a smile. "After all, you were the one who brought me here because you were not quite sure what to do, remember?"

"Yes, but …" Frank was cut off quickly.

"You hired me to get your key people trained on managing politics, and it wouldn't be right if I left here before giving you—the company's key person—a political makeover," Liz stood up. "You do realize that corporate culture is like the manure on my uncle's farm, don't you? It all rolls downhill eventually."

"Now there's an image I'll spend the rest of the night trying to forget," Frank grumbled. "Are you saying that all of these political problems from people like Dirk and Rani are my fault?"

"In a sense, yes." Liz was direct. She proceeded to explain the GUST approach to handling politics, and how each team member had applied the concepts to his or her individual problem.

"Wow, I had no idea it was that bad," he admitted.

"Of course you didn't, Frank. Many executives take their eye off the ball until it is too late—which would've been the case if Dirk had gotten his way. By the way, you owe Isabella, Josh, and Dee bonuses for uncovering exactly what Dirk was going to do in this meeting so we could resolve it. Josh's acting job in that board room was worthy of an Academy Award."

"Duly noted, Liz, but I can't babysit every employee. How can I tell who's playing nice and who is being a political snake?" Frank did not like being told he wasn't good at something.

"Throw them a CURVE, Frank." Liz's response left him a little irritated. Why did she always have to talk in riddles? She didn't leave him hanging for long, as she walked over to his whiteboard and wrote the following:

Executive Role in Managing Office Politics
Communication
Unity
Rewards
Values
Example

"Why did I know this was somehow going to be turned back on me?" he grinned. "OK, OK, explain. I know you've been dying to do this since you arrived here."

"It's simple, Frank. Every single person in your company is watching you. And these are the five things they are observing the most. They are also the five things they are using to determine what they and others can and cannot get away with.

"First is **Communication**. Every message, every hallway conversation, every email, every notice from HR … everything this company produces has your name on it, either directly or implied. The snake politicians are looking for loopholes and ways to use your communication to their own advantage. The ostrich politicians are probably just shrugging and hiding. The bear politicians are figuring out how to go on the defensive against the other two."

"So, how do I communicate in this company without offending somebody?" Frank seemed genuinely perplexed.

"Who said anything about not offending people?" Liz cocked her head at Frank in an inquisitive manner. "All I said is that everything you communicate has both an obvious text and an implied subtext, and that people are watching it and interpreting it for their own means. If your communication needs greater clarity, that's for you to determine. Of all the people in this company, you are the primary owner of the *REV*:Elation brand, Frank. With that comes the responsibility of defining what brand ownership should look like for others in this company."

"Fair enough," admitted Frank. "This next one ought to be

good."

"**Unity**?" inquired Liz. "What's so hard about that?"

"OK, so after all these months here, you think it's easy to get everybody agreeing on every point?" Frank looked at Liz as if she were speaking a different language.

"Has anyone ever told you that you assume way too much?" Liz responded in a tone only a true friend could get away with. "A pastor I know in Louisville always used to say that 'a man does not have to be my twin to be my brother.' Getting people to agree on everything is not what unity is about—that's not even realistic. However, providing a unified direction for your employees to follow can be a helpful start in ensuring that office politics are mitigated."

"Meaning what exactly?" Frank was not going to make this easy.

"Have you even communicated your company's mission and vision to everybody in a way that is meaningful? Do they know what the company's goals and objectives are?"

"We have a mission statement on a plaque in the lobby," defended Frank proudly. "It's done in bronze and mounted on marble. Looks great!"

"Yeah, you and every other company," Liz retorted. "And I've read it. It's not a mission statement. It's a mission essay. There's no way anyone could reasonably digest it and convert it to action. I'd suggest a little work on that front if you want to achieve unity at **REV**:Elation. This is old school, Frank. Nothing new here. Management theorists for decades, from Mary Parker Follett in the early 20th century all the way up to Deming during the Quality and TQM craze, have been supporting the idea of getting people on board with overarching goals that supersede petty conflicts."

"Moving right along …" Frank coaxed for Liz to continue, impatient now that he had digested her last comment and wanted to keep going.

"The next two are tied together," she began. "Are your

Rewards tied to what you as a company really **Value**?"

"Why do you think we have one of the industry's best pay-for-performance systems? Our raises and bonuses are all based on the actions and outcomes of our top performers," Frank recited this proudly from memory.

"OK, Frank, that speaks volumes. You've just told me that teamwork doesn't matter at all here at **REV**:Elation. What does matter is what the individual does."

"Teamwork matters here! We have slogans all over the place touting the benefits of teamwork. We send our employees to the best teamwork training that money can buy. We could cover a football field with all of the teamwork and motivational posters we have hanging up around here." Frank was genuinely upset at Liz's accusation.

"Ooh, lip service. Very impressive," Liz drawled sarcastically. "Do you reward teams? Do you provide bonuses based on team performance? Do teams receive recognition at quarterly performance events? Are teams allowed to make decisions? Are teams empowered to do what is right for their projects?" Liz was accustomed to this line of questioning to prove a point.

"Well, no. We reward individuals and we let individuals make decisions." Frank hated admitting that Liz was right once again.

"Frank, if you truly value teamwork, then you'll have to let the rewards follow that model. Otherwise, your employees will view it as little more than another instance of your talking the talk, but not walking the walk, and you will continue to get the same dysfunctional behavior out of your people. You may want to consider other so-called values your company employs, such as myopic rule-following and resource hoarding."

"And last but not least?" Frank was starting to see that even a seasoned executive still had a lot to learn.

"**Example** is so obvious that I shouldn't even have to explain it," Liz stated objectively. "Leading by example is in virtually every management textbook and leadership book to hit the shelves. People can't hear you when your actions keep drowning out your words, Frank. It's a known fact that our actions carry so much more weight than our words. That applies across all organizations and industries. Saint Francis of Assisi once admonished people to 'Preach the Gospel at all times. If necessary, use words.' Even he understood the importance of aligning results with observable action. Executives from more recent history such as Herb Kelleher at Southwest Airlines have personified this point vividly. As I told you months ago, Frank, you're a bright man. You get all of this corporate stuff. You enjoy it. You've just needed a little course correction."

"I suppose even an old dog like me can get off track and require retraining," chuckled Frank.

"Yes, and watch the 'old dog' comments; we are the same age, after all," chided Liz playfully. "I'm meeting my team for coffee at that jazz bar down the street. Would you like to join the masses for a well-deserved celebration and show them that you're starting to practice a few of these principles?"

"Sure," Frank responded as Liz started for the door. "I'll just be a minute. Go on. I'll catch up to you in the lobby."

As Frank closed up shop in his office, he looked around. Today was full of many victories. *REV*:Elation's newest product was destined to launch successfully. His worst political foe had been eliminated. Some of his top employees were now considerably more savvy about handling office politics than they had been a few months ago.

So why was he suddenly feeling like he still had a lot more work ahead of him than he had at the beginning of the day? He shrugged, shut off the light, and closed the door. Tomorrow would inevitably bring the answers to that question, as well as many more questions. For tonight at least, Frank was going to celebrate what was going right.

Epilogue

"It's hard to believe it's been a year!" Anne hugged Liz as she walked into her office. "And look at you! That cruise paid off. You look so relaxed and refreshed!"

"Well, I still can't believe you switched departments within **REV**:Elation after that amazing promotion you engineered for yourself," Liz lauded. "It's exciting that your Human Resources department finally added an Employee Relations division to help counsel and negotiate political conflicts."

"You seem to have planted those seeds in Frank's head, Liz," admitted Anne. "The GUST approach to managing politics has a huge demand across all divisions within **REV**:Elation. Even some of our customers and suppliers have noticed the difference in our culture and are asking for assistance. I'm amazed how fast my schedule fills up with requests for workshops on effective handling of office politics. It seems nobody is immune from it."

"Well, I am amused that, of everybody with whom I worked at **REV**:Elation, my biggest skeptic became my most devoted disciple," Liz chuckled.

"Yes, I'm almost ashamed when I look back—I was so afraid to even engage in politics when we first met," said Anne sheepishly.

"You were pretty gun-shy," agreed Liz. "Although I'm still surprised that after all the work you did to get promoted, and then to advance to Eve's boss on top of it all … you actually blind-sided me when you called and told me that you were leaving your sought-after position to get **REV**:Elation back on track with how they manage office politics."

"While I thought that having Eve as a boss was a disaster, having her as a subordinate was worse. She's just not a nice person. And to think that the reason she had it in for me all that time was something so petty."

"Oh?" Liz's eyebrow raised. "You never did tell me you had found out the reason behind the animosity."

"Get this," Anne became visibly animated. "The reason she hated me so much was that her ex-husband had left her years earlier for a woman whose first name also happened to be Anne. It was all a case of misplaced aggression. Go figure."

Liz shook her head in disbelief. Just when she thought she'd seen it all, there was always a new twist on corporate life to surprise her.

"Would you like a tour of the department?" Anne changed the subject. "It's a bit of a mess since we just moved. Shay actually helped us improve that situation a little. After Laurie Traiger was fired, Shay was asked to replace her. He's really taken the Help Desk to new levels, and procurements have never run more smoothly in this company. I haven't had as much of a chance to get things as organized around here as I would like since I've just returned from my vacation."

"I'd love to look around," exuded Liz, thrilled at the invitation.

The first room they visited was the department meeting room. There, displayed visibly on the wall opposite the row of windows, was the poster:

Office Politics 101
Game
Understand
Strategy
Take Action

"Nice touch," noted Liz, looking at the poster. "Wherever did you come up with such a clever acronym?"

"GUST has become the lifeblood of this department … and this organization," Anne said, smiling at Liz's reference. "It amazes me how many different departments and divisions struggle with politics, and how many corporate cultures let it bog them down."

"I knew your team would find it a helpful device," shared Liz. "I just didn't realize how marketable that part of my experience was. You've done a masterful job of turning it into a very successful technique to help your whole company solve its political problems."

"We've changed the approach a little from when you first presented it to our team here at *REV*:Elation. You were focused more on helping our direct team be successful, and therefore helping Frank be successful. Our approach starts with corporate culture, values, and mission. This helps remove some of the finger pointing that is inherent with corporate politics. We get people to realize that they're all in the same BOAT—or Balanced Organizational Alignment Triangle."

"Yes, you started telling me about that on the phone. I want to hear the details on this," Liz coaxed.

Anne took a page from Liz's playbook and turned to a nearby flip chart page, on which she drew and labeled a triangle:

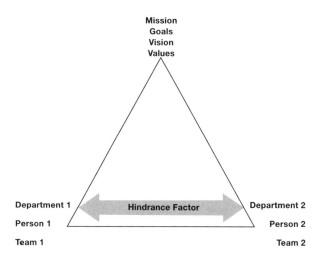

"Naturally, every organization is made up of individuals, departments, teams, divisions ... you name it," began Anne. "What we discovered after just a few workshops is that a major root cause of conflict is lack of alignment to a common goal, mission, value, or vision—both within a single department or team and sometimes across teams or departments."

"Like hidden agendas or inconsistent goals?" Liz clarified.

"Exactly," Anne confirmed. "The further away each entity—each department or team or individual—is from the common goal or mission, the further away they naturally drift from each other. The geometry of the triangle was the perfect way to demonstrate this phenomenon. We start by seeing how closely aligned they are to the organization's mission, vision, values, and goals."

"Let me guess, most people and departments aren't even aware that a direction exists." Reminded of her final discussion with Frank, Liz saw where this was going and was not surprised when Anne nodded in agreement to Liz's assessment.

"Exactly! So with no sail on the boat, it becomes very easy to see why two organizational entities drift apart. When I draw their specific triangle for them, it becomes very obvious why they are having many of their political battles. The distance between the two entities is labeled the hindrance factor, of which the level of politics played is a consideration. The higher the hindrance factor number, the greater the distance between the entities, and the more office politics will be played. That revelation then paves the way for the GUST approach." Anne was obviously proud of taking Liz's work a step further.

"Absolutely brilliant, Anne!" Liz was genuinely excited by the level of analysis and thought that had gone into this model. "But what happens if one entity is in alignment, but another is not?"

"Great question, Liz. And it's one that I get a lot at our workshops. As they say, a picture is worth a thousand words," Anne said as she drew a second diagram:

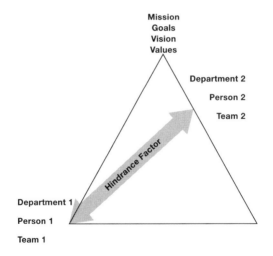

"So the size of the hindrance factor really doesn't change much unless both entities are in alignment," Liz surmised as Anne demonstrated with the final drawing:

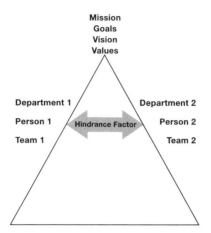

"This is really what an effective organization should look like," stated Anne. "The closer the alignment you have with the really important things in the organization, the fewer hindrances there will be to achieving them. There will always be disagreements; no organization can eliminate them totally. However, in an organization where all entities are in the same BOAT, those disagreements are generally easier to resolve since the higher end goals dominate."

"When can I sit in on one of your workshops?" Liz asked eagerly. "It sounds like Frank made a good decision in creating this division and putting you in charge."

Anne blushed as Isabella Gonzalez popped her head in the door. "I'm sorry to interrupt, Anne, but the manufacturing department is in desperate need of a political intervention. Can you talk to them? Oh, hi, Liz! Good to see you back here for a visit."

"Thanks, Isabella," Anne responded. Then turning to Liz, she asked, "Do you mind if I deal with this request?"

"Not at all!" Liz confirmed as Anne started for the door. "Please do. I'll be fine. I blocked off the whole afternoon for us to talk."

As Anne and Isabella walked away to address the needs of the latest department, Liz stood up. She looked around the office, and felt a strong surge of pride that Anne had come this far. The Anne Ericsen she had met a year ago was long gone. In her place was an enlightened and energized professional success story.

"Tale" Wind One

CHARACTER MAP	
Frank Truman	*The leader of the organization is the one who should be paying closest attention to corporate politics.*
Vic Elliott	*Allowing yourself to become a victim of politics sometimes leaves you with no choice but to leave the company.*
Liz Meredith	*Don't rest on your laurels—that should be the mantra of any shrewd corporate politician.*
Dirk Runnells	*Some executives never grow out of childhood and try to bully their way to the top through brute intimidation.*
Anne Ericsen	*A repressed individual's reluctance to engage in politics potentially can be very damaging.*
Eve Uhlwich	*Not every politician is evil, but there are those who are just rotten to the core ... and you have no idea why.*
Dee Connors	*Some team players can be a little overzealous, and their abrasive nature may turn off those who might be allies.*
Mark Washington	*There are politicians who protect their territory, afraid that any change is an invasion on their turf.*

Josh Matthews	*Covering one's bases is always good, but it's important to prepare for political contingencies as well.*
Isabella Gonzalez	*On every team, there's one individual who carries the load to get things done and doesn't want anything in the way.*
Michael Vanderpol	*Stonewalling and confusion are characteristic of some corporate politicians—to the regret of those around them.*
Shay Pradhan	*Not averse to politics, but also not wanting to take sides, this individual wants to maintain a neutral stance.*
Laurie Traiger	*Disorganized and overworked, this chaos-monger doesn't have time to do it right so she simply tries to cover her tail.*
Rani Blackburg	*Some consultants wear out their welcome and burrow into the organization just because they can.*

"Tale" Wind Two
GUST Quick Reference Guide

The Heart of GUST
Game
Understand
Strategy
Take Action

GAME

Identify what is being manipulated:

- Resources—time, money, organizational structures, systems, or other territorial ground

- Information—facts, data, perceptions, flow

- People—relationships, control, balance of power, communication, or anything that impacts how people interact or to whom they report.

UNDERSTAND

Motivations:

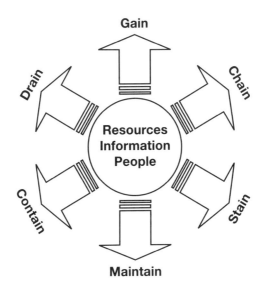

Gain – To add to, to obtain or procure

Chain – To bring together two unrelated things

Stain – To harm, undermine, injure, or discredit

Maintain – To keep the same, to prevent change

Contain – To hold onto, to not allow to exit or leave

Drain – To take away from, to steal or deplete

The "RIPPLE Effect" of Influence	
Reprimand	*punishment*
Incentive	*reward*
Position	*authority from title held or perceived*
Personality	*charisma or "likability"*
Liaison	*derived from association with power*
Expert	*knowledge or understanding*

STRATEGY

Political Strategy: RACE	
Roles	*Is your opponent a snake, ostrich, or bear?*
Approach	*overt or covert*
Character	*your own and your opponent's*
Evidence	*document everything in writing*

Strategies for handling each type of politician:

Snake	Ostrich	Bear
Cover your tail ... always	*Stress the importance of engaging and the impacts to the team*	*Act logically and ethically*
Share only necessary information; don't provide too much ammo they can use against you later	*Address fears and help overcome them*	*Balance facts and data with relationships & communication*
Consider the snake's allies and channels of communication; watch how you talk around their friends	*Provide a safe environment to express and vent*	*Show the bear you have their team's interest at heart, too*
	Don't force into a corner; keep them at ease	*Point to the big picture*

Take Action:

Taking Action - STOP to go	
Support	*Who is on your side?*
Timing	*Can you stall or do you need to act fast?*
Outcome	*What's the end goal?*
Passion	*Do you care enough to fight for it?*

Strategies for Executives:

Executive Role in Managing Office Politics	
Communication	*the executive's brand*
Unity	*Is everyone on the same page?*
Rewards	*What is motivating the behavior? Are the right behaviors being rewarded?*
Values	*What is important?*
Example	*Do your actions and words align?*

STEP 1: GAME

Identify the game ball that is being manipulated (note – it may fall into more than one category):

Resources	Information	People

STEP 2: UNDERSTAND

Identify the players and how they fit into the game:

Name	Type of Politician	Motivation	Alignment
	Snake Ostrich Bear	Chain Stain Maintain Contain Drain Gain	Support You Against You Neutral Unknown
	Snake Ostrich Bear	Chain Stain Maintain Contain Drain Gain	Support You Against You Neutral Unknown
	Snake Ostrich Bear	Chain Stain Maintain Contain Drain Gain	Support You Against You Neutral Unknown

Have you considered and addressed each of the following for your office politics challenges?

Roles	Approach	Character	Evidence
Are the other players acting like snakes, ostriches, or bears?	What is the best approach for handling this situation: overt or covert?	Describe the character of the other players?	List artifacts and evidence that can help you.
What are their hot buttons? What is motivating them?	Can you provide other "players" with a heads up on your strategy or is surprise your best element?	Are their behaviors consistent with their reputations?	
How much influence do you have?		What can you do to maintain your character?	

Support	Timing	Outcome	Passion
See Step 2.	How quickly do you need to act?	What does the "end game" look like?	How important is the outcome to you?
Of those who support you, how can you leverage that support?	How quickly are the other players moving?	What will your relationships with other players look like when the game is over?	Does it energize you or exhaust you?
Of those who are against you, how can you effectively go on the defensive?	What external deadlines exist that impact your goals?	What constitutes a "win" for you?	
What can you find out about those who are neutral or "uncertain"?			

"Tale" Wind Four

There are a few nods of acknowledgment that need to be made:

Those who have studied management in the past half century recognize the RIPPLE effect mentioned on page 61 as an offshoot of the research that French and Raven published as "Studies in social power" in 1959 for the University of Michigan's Institute for Social Research (five power bases). I added Liaison as a means of influence based on my observations from networking and connecting with other professionals. While Raven added Connectivity and Information as power bases in 1993, connectivity was only recognized as creating compliance; however, current literature and personal experience has demonstrated that these "mavens" (as Gladwell calls them) have the power to built committed communities. (See http://www. strategyvectormodel.com/special_management_topics/Bases_of_ power.asp for more information.)

Bob Russell is the retired Head Pastor of Southeast Christian Church in Louisville, KY. He was the first person I heard use the phrase, "Man does not have to be my twin to be my brother" at the North American Christian Convention in 2003. His spiritual and social influence continue to be felt across the globe.

These surveys are a tool to facilitate communication. They are not intended as a scientific instrument, but they can be used to track averages and trends.

Tips for Administering These Surveys

- Add your own questions as you see fit for any of the three surveys.

- The surveys may be completed anonymously (recommended if you perceive a lack of trust in your organization) or with open dialogue.

- Capture a baseline score (no matter how painful it is). Then revisit the survey after you've had a chance to correct some of the issues uncovered. Compare the two scores and celebrate.

- Find a neutral party to collect and tabulate the surveys. Try to avoid an individual associated with any one division or department.

- Watch for differences in perceptions among employees, managers, and executives. This is a red flag that there is trouble.

- Keep an open mind if problems surface. People will tell you what's really going wrong if and only if you listen with your heart. Remain humble and be prepared to hear the worst (then you might be pleasantly surprised). Finally, attack problems, not people (bad people almost always eventually attack themselves anyway).

Employee BOAT Survey

Mark each question on a scale of 1 to 5	1 strongly disagree	2 disagree	3 neutral	4 agree	5 strongly agree
I know my company's mission statement					
I understand my company's mission statement					
I know my division/ department/team's mission statement					
I understand my division/ department/team's mission statement					
There are clear objectives for performance communicated to my division/department/team					
I understand the objectives for my division/department/team and how to achieve them					
My division/department/team's mission and objectives align with my company's mission and objectives					
There are clear objectives communicated for my personal performance					
I understand how to achieve the objectives for my personal performance					
The rewards for my division/department/team's performance clearly align with the objectives					
The rewards for my personal performance clearly align with my objectives					
I can identify other divisions/ departments/teams and how they relate to my own					

I know how other individuals' work relates to my own outcomes					
My department/division/team's objectives align with and do not contradict that of others					
The goals of the people in my department align with the goals of the department					
I spend more of my time doing productive work than I do engaging in unproductive political behavior					
I perceive that my manager supports my goals as well as those of my department/division/team					
Whenever there is a conflict, department or division goals override individual goals					
Whenever there is a conflict, organizational mission and goals override department or division goals					

Manager BOAT Survey

Mark each question on a scale of 1 to 5	1 strongly disagree	2 dis-agree	3 neutral	4 agree	5 strongly agree
I know my company's mission statement and goals					
I understand my company's mission statement and goals					
I know my division/department/team's mission statement					
I understand my division/department/team's mission statement					
I've communicated my division/department/team's mission and objectives and goals to my staff					
There are clear objectives for performance communicated to my division/department/team					
I understand the objectives for my division/department/team and how to achieve them					
My division/department/team's mission and objectives align with my company's mission and objectives					
There are clear objectives communicated for my personal performance					
I understand how to achieve the objectives for my personal performance					
The rewards for my division/department/team's performance clearly align with the objectives					
The rewards for my personal performance clearly align with my objectives					
My staff knows and understands the company's mission statement					

My staff knows and understands the company's objectives and goals					
My staff knows and understands the department/division/team's mission statement					
My staff knows and understands the department/division/team's objectives and goals					
My staff knows and understands their own objectives and goals, how to achieve them, and what rewards they receive for performance					
I can identify other divisions/departments/teams and how they relate to my own					
I know how other individuals' work relates to my own outcomes					
My department/division/team's objectives align with and do not contradict that of others					
The goals of the people in my department align with the goals of the department					
I spend more of my time doing productive work than I do engaging in unproductive political behavior					
I perceive that my manager supports my goals as well as those of my department/division/team					
Whenever there is a conflict, department or division goals override individual goals					
Whenever there is a conflict, organizational mission and goals override department or division goals					

Executive (VP and C-Level) BOAT Survey

Mark each question on a scale of 1 to 5	1 strongly disagree	2 disagree	3 neutral	4 agree	5 strongly agree
I know my company's mission statement and goals					
I understand my company's mission statement and goals					
I know my division's mission statement					
I understand my division's mission statement					
I've communicated the company's mission and objectives to my division's managers					
I've communicated my division's mission, objectives, and goals to my managers					
There are clear objectives for performance communicated to my division					
I understand the objectives for my division and how to achieve them					
My managers understand the objectives for my division and how to achieve them					
My division's mission and objectives align with my company's mission and objectives					
There are clear objectives communicated for my personal performance					
I understand how to achieve the objectives for my personal performance					
The rewards for my division's performance clearly align with the objectives					

The rewards for my personal performance clearly align with my objectives					
My managers know and understand the company's mission statement					
My managers know and understand the company's objectives and goals					
My managers know and understand the division's mission statement					
My managers know and understand the division's objectives and goals					
My managers know and understand their own objectives and goals, how to achieve them, and what rewards they receive for performance					
I can identify other divisions and how they relate to my own					
My division's objectives align with and do not contradict that of others					
The goals of employees and managers in my division align with the goals of my division					
I spend more of my time doing productive work than I do engaging in unproductive political behavior					
I support the goals of my division and those of the managers within my division					
Whenever there is a conflict, department or division goals override individual goals					
Whenever there is a conflict, organizational mission and goals override department or division goals					

About the Author

Timothy L. Johnson is the Chief Accomplishment Officer of Carpe Factum, Inc. (formerly Delta Project Solutions). Two decades of experience in project management, systems thinking, business analysis, and team facilitation have culminated in a laser-focused mission to help organizations "seize the accomplishment." His roles as consultant, coach, and college instructor have exposed him to numerous cultures and behaviors. His work on myriad projects of varying sizes for multiple organizations allows him to help organizations and individuals identify and manage the factors that help and hinder achieving the accomplishments for which they are destined.

Timothy is available for executive coaching, keynote speeches, and workshops. You many find out more about his services, as well as read his blog, at his website, www.carpefactum.com. Timothy is also a regular contributor to www.office-politics.com. He resides in Des Moines, Iowa with his family.